PROTECT YOURSELF

The complete guide to safeguarding your life and home

By N.H. and S.K. MAGER

A Dell/Benjamin Company Book

"PROTECT YOURSELF"

Chapter 1

It Can't Happen to Me

But then one evening while we were out, it did happen . . .

Our home was burglarized! OUR HOME! Let me tell you it was a shattering experience — hassling with the insurance company, our lingering anxiety, the memory of belongings pawed through, strewn about. ("It could have been worse. Thank God our daughter wasn't home sleeping . . .")

Last week a neighbor came home from vacation to a scene of appalling vandalism. House broken into. Upstairs bathtub plugged, the water left running. Freezer full of meat standing wide open. Soft drinks dumped into the piano and color TV. Mindless ruin to the tune of thousands of dollars!

Can't happen to you? Look around your home. Can burglars get in by breaking a window or prying a door lock? You'll probably find entry is simple even for an amateur.

"Luckily, I Live in a Safe Neighborhood . . ."

The safe neighborhoods of yesterday . . . suburbia . . . are the areas experiencing the greatest growth of break-ins today. That's where people with above-average incomes congregate. Their affluence means more personal possessions, more TVs, more jewelry, more stamp and coin collections . . . and more crime incentive. Intruders search out these areas (many of the intruders are local youngsters well aware of the promise of easy loot) because the return per break-in is higher than anywhere else in town. Even smaller cities and rural areas are being plagued by a rapid rise in crime and burglaries.

"I Have a Dog" . . . "We Have a Gun" . . . "I Can Take Care of Myself . . ."

Forget the deterrent value of a dog, unless you are willing to live with a specially trained "killer" attack dog (and the legal consequences if he harms someone). As for Rover, the family pet, a tasty bone can quickly silence him, or he can be let loose to roam outside while the burglar loots the inside.

As for guns, they can be trouble, and little protection. Most intruders take pains to avoid you, and strike only when they know you are gone. Once they're in, that gun is apt to disappear along with the TV set, portable radios, jewelry, and other easily fenced possessions. Consider, too, the consequences of confronting a burglar. He may have a gun and shoot first. The law may charge you with a crime if you shoot an unarmed intruder. His presence on your premises doesn't give you the license to kill him, and would you want to live with such a memory if you did act in haste? Guns are inherently dangerous and can too easily get into the hands of children. Most handguns and rifles will penetrate walls and could easily injure someone beyond. The police themselves will tell you: guns are not the answer.

"We Really Have Nothing Worth Stealing . . ."

The intruder may not be convinced of that until he has ransacked your home, dumped out all dresser drawers, emptied all closets, slashed furniture cushions and mattresses. Or he's apt to become so frustrated that he vandalizes your home in venting his feelings. This senseless destruction of your things can cause you greater pain than the loss of any possession.

"I'm Protected With Insurance . . ."

Think so? Say you bought your color TV two years ago for $500, and you find it stolen. How much do you think you'll get from your insurance company? $350, perhaps $400, but not the price of *replacement*. And what with inflation, that set will probably now cost $600 or more to replace. You're out hundreds of dollars in spite of insurance. Or, stolen items may well be family heirlooms that cannot be replaced at any price. The loss or malicious destruction of items such as grandfather clocks, sterling serving pieces, and other treasures of sentimental value can be far more painful than the loss of a color TV.

"OK . . . But I Still Don't Think It Will Happen to Me . . ."

Actually, chances are alarmingly high that you will be hit. Crime experts report that within five years *one out of every five* American homes will be burglarized. Last year 45 million families fell victim to more than 12 million crimes, including theft, burglary, assault, robbery, rape and murder. This rate of crime grows rapidly year by year, outstripping even the growth in population.

Look at the frightening record covering just one year:

Murders — 20 thousand.

Forcible rape — over 56 thousand victims.

Robbery with violence or force — nearly half a million cases.

Aggravated assault — half a million.

Motor vehicle thefts — well over a million.

Burglaries — *3¼ million*!

Theft — about *6 million* reported.

Altogether this adds up to well over 11 million crimes. And the frightening fact is that one death in every hundred today is a homicide! The threat to home and loved ones is statistically clear.

In personal terms we must realize that in a single year five persons out of every hundred throughout the United States — men, women and children — are victims of some kind of crime. If we figure four members to a family, *one in every five families is victimized.* One in every sixteen is burglarized. One family in eight suffers some form of larceny. One family out of every fifty has its car stolen.

We think of deaths on the highway as alarming. Yet the fact is that there are as many reported rapes as auto deaths!

Every minute the toll mounts, faster and faster as crime outraces population growth.

"It can't happen to me?" It clearly can happen, and the odds suggest that there is every likelihood it will.

Can we predict who the victim will be?

Chance is the biggest element in determining who will be robbed, mugged or raped. Most criminals don't "select" a victim. They set out to commit a particular crime, but the victim in most instances will be determined by the whim of the moment.

The amount of incentive to carry out a crime plays an important part in the criminal's decision and determination. Thus, the purpose of this book is to show you HOW to make yourself *far more secure against this threat.* If you plan intelligently, you can greatly reduce the risks by providing increased safeguards for yourself and your property. The key is to know *what to do* and *how much protection* to provide at *a cost you can afford.*

And that, of course, is the reason for this book. To alert you, inform you, help you take the sensible steps that greatly add to your personal security. The threat of crime is increasing rapidly. In the matter of burglary alone, FBI crime reports show residential burglary up well over 50 percent in the last five years (56 percent during the seemingly secure daytime hours!). If crime continues to increase at the present rates, every family will have a 50/50 chance of being victimized *every year* by the year 2000.

Protecting Yourself

It is human nature for people to think, "It won't happen to me." Perhaps it is just as well to have a sort of built-in protective mechanism so we don't worry ourselves sick over all the hazards and "near misses" we encounter without incident each day of our lives.

Still, certain high-probability hazards *do exist*, along with the means to *guard ourselves against them.* Crime victimizes most heavily those people who lack the foresight to take steps to minimize their risk. These are the careless, the people who believe "it can't happen to me," the poor who can't afford precautions, and the "sales resistant" ones who simply refuse to invest even a modest amount of money in protection.

Your home is only as safe as its weakest point of entry. It is well worth the effort (and modest cost) to make such entry points sufficiently strong so the risk and effort needed to get in are so great that they will discourage the average burglar and make him look for an easier target.

In the chapters ahead, we will look at the ways you can make yourself more secure in all aspects of your life, and thus far less likely to become one of the ugly crime statistics during your lifetime.

Chapter 2

The Vulnerable Door

> *"There is no amount of protection afforded a home by locks on doors and windows that gives assurance that a person with criminal intent will be unable to gain entry. Nevertheless, protective devices can require a robber to spend considerable time and effort on the 'breaking and entering' job and if he thinks breaking into a house or apartment will be too difficult, he is likely to pass the premises by and choose the house or garage of someone else for his operations."*
>
> —Consumer Research Magazine
> January 1976

Doors are the natural entry points to your home. We all use them many times a day, to go in and out. No wonder that criminals also find them convenient to use in entering houses they intend to burglarize. The sad fact is that people all too frequently make it simple for the burglar by leaving doors unlocked or by having inadequate exterior doors and locks.

Since your front — and rear — doors are your first line of defense in providing security for your home, you'll want to take every reasonable precaution to make them as burglar-proof as possible. Weak, insufficient doors can be broken through. Cheap, shoddy locks can be forced or picked. But even the strongest door and the most elaborate and sophisticated lock will provide no protection if the door is carelessly left unlocked.

Doors Are for Locks

Locks for security were used by the Egyptians as far back as 1000 B.C. They were massive wooden bars with a hollow center in which wooden pins acted as bolts. The keys were twenty-four inches long, weighed four pounds, and were inserted into the inside lock through a hole in the door.

The Greeks invented the keyhole and were able to reduce the key to about twelve inches. By the time the Romans faced the home security problem, the key became a portable six to twenty-four inches for most doors, but some keys were worn on finger rings.

By the sixteenth century, an Englishman created a lock that would shackle anyone who tampered with it, gripping him with metal handcuffs. Later, doors were equipped with muskets that would fire on the intruder who didn't make the right motions. A forerunner of the modern alarm system was created in the eighteenth century and gave off a loud noise to alert the homeowner.

The first cylinder lock in the United States was made by Linus Yale, Jr. in 1861. Yale, the son of a locksmith, was an artist. What he produced was a miniature of the Egyptian model.

Lock That Door

Almost all home robberies begin with entrance through a door or a window. In many areas, doors remain unlocked so that children, animals, even neighbors can feel free to come in as they wish.

Learn to lock your door when you put out the garbage, pick up the mail, swap a piece of gossip with a neighbor, move the car, or check up on your child playing in the street or nearby playground.

Daytime Is Not Necessarily Safe Time

Daytime burglaries are on the increase. Just because it's light doesn't mean that criminals are all in hiding. On the contrary, daytime residence burglaries are on the same upswing as nighttime robberies. So it is just as important to make certain that you lock up even if you're leaving the house "just for a minute." With an unlocked door to tempt him, a burglar can be in and out in a very few minutes.

The charts that follow show the relationship of daytime to nighttime burglaries, and pinpoint the incidence of daylight crime.

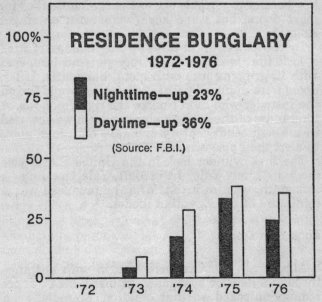

Yearly percentage of increase in residence burglaries

Myril Zion, who heads the famed M. Zion Company, surveyed the points of entry for several thousand burglaries. That study shows the relative danger and vulnerability of doors and windows, as follows:

Doors — Used by intruders in 80 percent of the instances

Front door — open or inadequate lock (42 percent)

— glass panels broken, allowing door to be unlocked (7 percent)

— use of key (2 percent)

Back door — glass panels broken and door unlocked (19 percent)

— open or inadequate lock (10 percent)

Windows — Used in 20 percent of the instances

— broken (9 percent)

— forced (6 percent)

— basement windows broken (5 percent)

Your Door Must Be Sturdy

Select a strong door, well fitted into a sturdy frame. A solid wooden door (at least 1¾ inch thick) or a metal door (with a hollow case) is best. If, for esthetic reasons, you select a door with wood or glass panels, make sure the panels are heavy and solid and are securely installed. Of the four kinds of doors — metal, solid wood, a frame with wood panels, and a hollow door with outside surface of thin veneer — only the metal door or a solid wooden door offer any real protection.

Glass is commonly used in doors to let light in and to permit the homeowner to see who is outside. Such a glass panel is an obvious weakness. An intruder can remove it and reach in to release the latch. You should replace glass panels with unbreakable plastic, or cover the panel with an attractive metal grillwork.

A strong fist can punch through a hollow wooden door. A panel door is only as good as the workmanship which determined how thick the panels are and how well they are put in place.

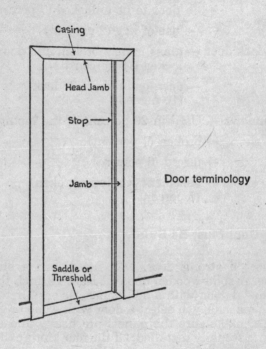

Door terminology

Even if the door was snug when the house was built, warping and settling may have allowed cracks to develop. If you find this to be true, replace the door or reinforce the frame. If you don't want to go to this expense, at least replace the locks so the bolts will slip into the frame for at least ¾ of an inch. Actually, a one-inch bolt should be the minimum.

Picking a lock requires some skill, but most burglars don't need to pick or blast out a lock. The jimmy is faster and, therefore, safer for the burglar. If breaking a glass panel doesn't work, the jimmy or an ordinary door jack can be inserted between the jamb and the edge of the door. With proper leverage, the door and the jamb can be forced apart, thus removing the bolt from the door plate.

Here are two ways you can prevent this: (1) Attach a thumb lock to the inside face of the door with a bolt of sufficient length or (2) attach an L-shaped metal strip to cover the crack between the door and frame. This may be attached to the frame or to the door on the side that swings outward. Don't use ordinary screws! These allow the burglar to remove the barrier. Use bolts or nonretractable screws, so that the strip cannot be removed easily.

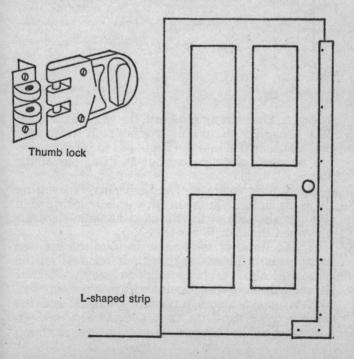

Thumb lock

L-shaped strip

Further Protection for Your Doors

All doors have hinges. If the door swings out, the hinges will be exposed. An intruder can quite easily remove the hinge pins and slip the door right out of the frame, unless you take steps to protect those exposed hinges. Three means of preventing this are illustrated below:

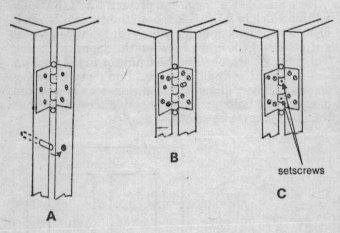

B

setscrews

C

A

Fig. A. Sink strong pins into the edge of the door, with enough of the pin protruding so it fits snugly into a hole drilled into the frame. Even if hinge pins are removed, the door cannot be lifted out of the frame.

Fig. B. A stronger use of such pins involves setting them through the hinge itself, with a hole drilled in the opposite side of the hinge to accommodate the pin when the door is closed.

Fig. C. Another solution is to weld the exposed hinge pins in place, making their removal all the more difficult. It is also possible to insert a setscrew through the hinge at a point which is not exposed.

Most outside doors have the doorstop and the jamb in one piece. Thus, the stop can't be sawed off. Inasmuch as the stop covers the space between jamb and door, the jimmy cannot be inserted. A well-fitted door is itself a protection.

Given time and skill, a thief can pass through your door like a genie. Your objective is to make it as difficult and time consuming as possible. This increases the danger of discovery for the thief. The idea is to make it not worth the thief's time, nor the risk to burglarize *your* home.

Door Locks

> *"Delaying a burglar for four minutes is generally considered sufficient to prevent entry into a house or apartment. A burglar wants to avoid being caught, so the longer it takes to force a door or window the greater his risk. The burglar wants to avoid making noise — like breaking glass or smashing doors — and he wants to avoid attracting attention. It is nearly impossible to make a house or apartment impregnable — but it is relatively easy and inexpensive to make forced entry difficult and to delay the burglar."*

> — The National Sheriffs' Association

There Are No Burglar-Proof Locks

"There are foolproof locks, but many burglars are not fools," says Sgt. Arthur H. Paholke of the Chicago Police Department.

That's why you never hear of a jammed bank-vault door being blasted open. Even so sophisticated a locking device can be violated by a talented locksmith. Given time and the proper tools, he can open the vault. Imagine how much simpler, then, for the talented burglar to gain entry to your home via front or back door, no matter how secure the locks!

Almost all locks can be picked by a professional. Indeed, if you lose your keys, your local police will probably tell you whom to call to pick your lock.

Fortunately, relatively few thieves take the pains to acquire skills as lock pickers. Virtually any lock can be picked; some just take longer than others. Time, of course, increases the criminal's risk.

The chief purpose of a lock is to buy time from a burglar. Time always works against his interests.

Locks provide only relative safety. As technology makes for stronger locks, thieves develop new ways to open them. The larger the probable haul, the more sophisticated the burglar who will be tempted.

Locks are a householder's first line of defense. The knowledgeable thief will try to circumvent the lock. If he succeeds, an alarm can call attention to his act and create noise that will frighten him off. That is why more and more homeowners are adding the back-up protection of an alarm system.

There are a number of different kinds of locks which provide varying amounts of protection for your exterior doors. Among the commonly found locks are those mounted in the door itself (bored or mortised) and those which are mounted on the surface of the door (rim locks).

Rim-mounted spring latch. Courtesy of Schlage

Key-in-Knob Spring Bolt. Inexpensive and easy to install, this lockset has a spring latch which automatically locks the door when it is closed. However, the spring-latch lock is easy to open without a key. It can be "shimmed" (disengaged with a thin piece of metal or wood pick) or pried open with a plastic card (a process called "loiding," from celluloid, a plastic which is often used in making such cards).

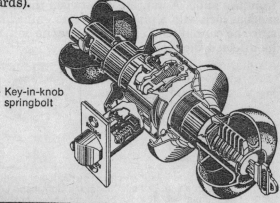

Key-in-knob springbolt

Top quality mortise lock has the usual bolt plus a deadbolt activated by thumb turn and externally by key. Screw locks cylinder in place, so it can't be pulled while door is shut.

Next step up the line, substantially more secure and more burglar-resistant, is the **mortise lock**. Instead of being simply pushed into a hole cut through the door, it is inset into a deep mortise from the edge of the door, thus the word *mortise* in its name. It eliminates, first of all, the possibility of opening by force applied to the doorknob. In the mortise lock, the lock cylinder is housed in a metal box separate from the knob. A burglar who twists the knob off a mortise lock with a pipe wrench has gained nothing since he cannot reach in to activate the bolt, nor has he affected the lock.

At left is a simple bolt which can be carded or pushed back with a wire or knife blade; the right hand bolt has plunger which locks bolt in extended position and prevents opening without a key.

With a deadlatch plunger, the spring bolt lock is not so vulnerable to shimming or being pried open. But because the latch bolt usually extends only a small distance into the strike plate (sometimes only ¼ inch or less) an energetic burglar can often jimmy the bolt out of the frame with a sturdy screwdriver.

A sharp hammer blow or a good twist with a wrench will often remove the knob from spring bolt locks. Because of this, it is a good idea to add a deadbolt lock to your exterior doors if you only have a spring bolt lock now.

Dead-Bolt Locks

A dead-bolt lock features a metal bolt which, when engaged, fits into the strike plate of the door frame (on a mortised lock) or into a separate metal housing on the frame (if a rim lock). The bolt has a square end, which is set in the locked position either by a second turn of the key or by a thumb knob on the interior side of the door. In addition to being more difficult to pick than a spring bolt lock, a dead-bolt lock makes jimmying the door relatively difficult. The better dead-bolt locks will have a cylinder guard ring made from hardened steel. The bolt itself will be of hardened steel, or will have a hardened steel pin inside the bolt, to prevent sawing.

Some dead-bolt locks have two cylinders — one for opening the door from inside the house, as well as one for opening from the outside. This system can frustrate a thief who breaks the glass panel on a door and reaches in to unlatch the bolt. Without the key, he can't open the door. And, even if he enters through a window, he can't exit through a door with your TV! But the dual key system also has its drawback for the family, because one needs a key to get out. In an emergency, a lost or misplaced key could be a tragic problem. If you install such a lock, be sure to leave the inside key in the lock when you're home, but remove it when you go out. Or you can put the key on a convenient nail far enough away from the door to prevent anyone from reaching in and grabbing it.

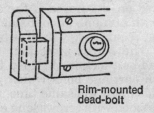

Rim-mounted
dead-bolt

Rim-Mounted Dead-Bolts

Any rim-mounted lock depends for security on the care with which it is mounted and on the quality of the door and frame where it is placed. If the screws are not long enough, or if they bite into soft or rotten wood, the lock may be strong but the door may very well give way to the resolute strength of a determined intruder.

The standard dead-bolt lock, with a rectangular bolt one inch long that closes into a mortised strike plate mounted in the door frame, cannot be shimmed or pried open. Of course, if the intruder demolishes the door frame in the process of kicking at the door, the lock won't hold.

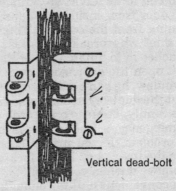

Vertical dead-bolt

The vertical dead-bolt lock ("drop-bolt") is an even better door guard. This "jimmy-resistant" lock is designed to engage vertical bolts in heavy metal rings mounted on the frame of the door. Drop-bolt locks come with a thumb knob inside or with double cylinders that require a key from either the inside or the outside. The surest protection from any rim-mounted dead-bolt lock is obtained from mounting the lock with carriage bolts which go all the way through the door. At the same time, the strike plate should be attached with screws long enough to reach into the studs which surround the door frame.

The Medeco cylinder is today's ultimate in lock cylinders readily available for residential protection. The design of the Medeco cylinder, with its variable angle cuts on the key, represents the first

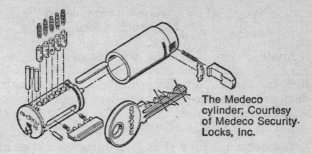

The Medeco cylinder; Courtesy of Medeco Security Locks, Inc.

major improvement in lock mechanisms since the development of the pin-tumbler lock. The Medeco cylinder is considered pickproof and is generally recognized as the finest on the market. Caution: this high-security cylinder, however, can offer no greater protection than the lock or door in which it is installed. Make sure these offer comparable protection.

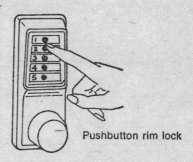

Pushbutton rim lock

Keyless locks, a relatively new development, are becoming more and more popular, though their very newness means that they have not been extensively tested. **The push-button rim lock** comes with a spring-latch bolt or a dead-bolt device. The combination can be changed quite easily, and the lock can be activated either by the combination or by a switch hidden at some distance from the door. While a combination lock is virtually impossible to pick, it can of course be opened by anyone who may learn the combination. If you purchase such a lock, be sure that the bolt is long enough to fasten the door securely.

Another type of keyless lock features a magnetic card or plastic identification device. Although the lock is, strictly speaking, keyless, the unlocking device must still be carried and used to open the lock. An electronic system "reads" the information encoded in the card, and activates the lock.

The **buttress lock** (Fox lock) includes a steel bar attached to the door and the floor as an angular brace. It may also have a dead-bolt of as much as two inches into the doorjamb. The appearance is distressing to some, but the security is comforting. The bar can be removed for appearance's sake when one has visitors.

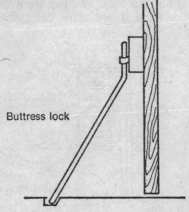

Buttress lock

Chain locks are recommended for your door as a precaution, provided you do not rely on them totally. A professional thief can cut a chain with a bolt cutter in a few seconds or even with a hacksaw, if time is available. Many chain locks are installed with screws so short that the door can be kicked in by the average man. Use screws at least 1¼ inches long to set into live wood so that they are well anchored.

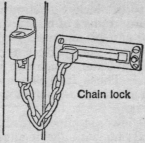

Chain lock

A chain lock with a key lock is safer than the ordinary bolt. A practiced thief can open an ordinary lock with a piece of tape, a rubber band, and a paper clip. However, chain locks are useful for several purposes. If you are not at home, they may suggest to an illegal entrant that someone *is* at home. In any case, a chain lock adds to the time necessary to gain entry. If you are at home, it gives you an opportunity to check out a caller, even if you think you know who is ringing the bell, and to speak to someone without opening the door completely. However, a peephole and speaking device are better for such a purpose.

Use chain lock to check on visitors

Don't leave a door open on a chain lock "for ventilation," as it takes only a few seconds to snap the chain with a bolt cutter.

Many old homes, most hotel rooms, and some apartments have a **night latch** which is, in effect, an extra bolt to the lock. Sometimes these can be opened by sliding a piece of plastic or a credit card into the gap or can be removed by prying out the faceplate, removing the cylinder and disengaging the lock. A key-in-knob device can be pried loose with a crowbar. These latches may deter an intruder, but you should not depend totally on them if you can avoid it.

A peephole viewer is important. But be sure you invest in a good one, with a wide-angled (180°) field of vision. Inexpensive ones with a limited viewing field will not always permit you to see who is at the door. Peephole viewers are one-directional only; there is no danger of anyone's looking into your room from the outside.

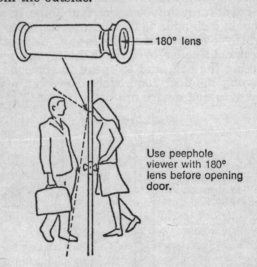

180° lens

Use peephole viewer with 180° lens before opening door.

Screen Doors and Storm Doors

Keep your screen door locked, even if the main door is also locked. That way, if you must open the door to see who is outside, you still have some protection. You can quickly close the front door if necessary.

Storm doors are fine for keeping the cold out, but they offer practically no protection against an intruder. A screwdriver is often enough to provide entrance through a storm door.

The Back Door

Because a back door can't be seen from the street, it is often a prime target for an intruder. If there is a glass panel, it can rather easily be smashed, offering an intruder an easy reach to an inside knob. A decorative but sturdy metal grille over the glass will offer some protection. Heavy gauge slide bolts at the top and bottom of the door will provide additional security.

A back door or a side door needs especially good locks — at least as good as the locks on your front door. An inexpensive way of securing a back door when you are going away or at night is by mounting two metal brackets on the door frame and inserting a 2″ x 4″ bolt, but this is useless if a glass panel can be broken to allow the bolt to be removed.

Sliding Glass Doors

Sliding doors are particularly vulnerable. Suburban homes and some apartments often have them opening onto an easily accessible patio. In fact, sliding glass doors are probably the first target an intruder will try. Many panels can be lifted off their tracks and removed. The standard locks are flimsy and a screwdriver, in most cases, can pry them open. Substantial locks that fit into the top or bottom track are an important addition to security. One commonly used device is a length of dowel or rod in the slide track. This offers little protection, however, because the rod can be pried loose or the door can be lifted right off the track. A better solution is to drill a hole through the frame and the track at the bottom of the door. A bolt lock placed through the hole will prevent the door from being slid open or lifted out.

A patio door bar, which folds down to a horizontal position across the center of the door, prevents the sliding portion from being opened. It is good security, not only because of its effectiveness in keeping the door closed, but also because it is visible to an intruder and tells him that you care about the security of your home.

Any sliding-door locking device can be frustrated by breaking the glass in the door. But while a burglar might break small windows, most will hesitate to break an entire glass door, which can be both dangerous and noisy.

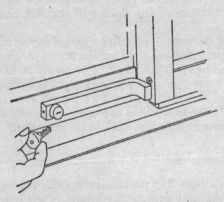

Typical patio door lock

The Garage

The most hazardous of doors that lead into your house is the door between the garage and the house. Once the intruder is in your garage, he is out of sight from the street. He can take as much time as he needs and he generally finds all the tools needed nearby.

Whether or not your garage offers entry into your house, it should be locked at all times, if only to protect your car and the other valuables stored there. Even if there is no door to your house, the garage may offer an opportunity for a wall to be broken as a means of entry into the house. The door between an inside garage and a home is often flimsy — a hollow door or one with panels. This is a particularly vulnerable spot, because the garage offers concealment to an intruder.

Lighting between an unattached garage and your house should be sufficient to make a person visible for at least thirty feet on a dark night. The inside of the garage should have at least a 100-watt bulb which lights up when the door is opened.

Keep your garage uncluttered so that a thief does not find it convenient as a hiding place.

The automatic (radio controlled) garage door is not only a convenience but a good security device. It saves you the trouble and potential danger of getting out of the car to open the garage when you return at night or closing the door when you leave at any time.

Automatic doors are made so they may also be opened with a key or by pressing a button either inside or outside the house. Bear in mind that you should be able to open the door from inside the garage. The door may also be locked with a key when you are away.

If your garage has a window, it is a good idea to opaque it, so a passerby cannot see if your car is in the garage or not. An empty garage is usually a signal that you are not home.

The Extra Ounce of Protection

Although locks and doors are your first (and very important) lines of defense, they cannot do the job alone, 100 percent of the time. Locks *can* by picked or forced; doors *can* be jimmied or broken through. An unoccupied house, in the dark of night, offers long uninterrupted hours for a determined intruder to break in.

So after you have made sure that your doors and locks are as completely strong and thoroughly thief-proof as possible, you should consider an extra measure of protection, a dependable alarm system. Intruders dare not remain on the premises when a noisy alarm tells the whole neighborhood that something is going on in your house. Recent technological advances mean that alarm systems need not be expensive nor difficult to install. We'll examine some of the newest systems available to homeowners in chapter 4.

Chapter 3

The Vulnerable Window

If the doors in your home are relatively secure, the chances are that an intruder will turn his attention to your windows. Some are more vulnerable than others and therefore likely entry points for an intruder.

All Windows Should Be Protected

Readily accessible ground-level windows obviously need extra protection and should be the first to be checked. Windows on the upper floors of homes are often viewed as inaccessible and, therefore, as not requiring security measures. This is a fallacy, particularly when there are trees or buildings nearby. Every window in a house should be securely locked and protected.

Windows above ground level are less of a temptation to an intruder than ground-level windows. However, they may be accessible by way of fire escapes, porches, garage roofs or the roofs of neighboring buildings, trees, or a handy ladder. Where buildings are close together, a plank has been known to be used. Some professional thieves have even lowered themselves from one apartment sun porch to another in the search for open windows and doors. If you have an outside ladder, don't leave it where it can be found by a visiting thief. Lock it in the garage or tool shed. Chain it to a fixed part of the building. Do not invite a thief to use it by making it accessible or visible, but remember also that a thief often brings his own ladder.

Protecting Your Windows

Windows come in a variety of sizes, shapes, and types, and each presents its own security problem. The most common window, and the most vulnerable, is the sliding **double-hung** window, where one or both of two panels will slide up and down or sideways. These windows are fastened with a "butterfly" lock, which can generally be opened by the most amateurish of thieves. All it takes is a long blade of metal, inserted between the two frames. Prying up on the latch forces it away from the flange, unlocking the window. A sophisticated version of the butterfly latch, which closes with a key, is illustrated here. This locking mechanism prevents the window from being opened, even if the glass is broken.

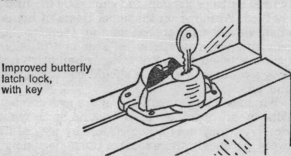

Improved butterfly
latch lock,
with key

An improved version of the standard sash lock is the "Griptite" model, which pulls the two window frames together when the latch is closed. There is not enough space to work a knife blade or other metal strip between the frames to unlock the latch. This type of latch also has a snap-lock device that keeps the two pieces together despite vigorous shaking or banging on the window frames.

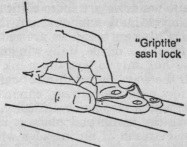

"Griptite" sash lock

A more sophisticated type of lock is the "ventilation lock." For greatest protection, get the type that is key operated. The big advantage of a ventilation lock is the ability to lock a window in place while it is not entirely closed. The ordinary ventilation lock can lock a window at a closed position or at one partly opened position.

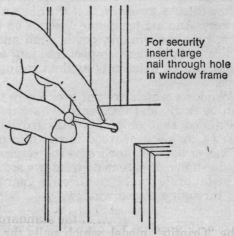

For security insert large nail through hole in window frame

Double-hung windows can also be secured by a large nail or bolt inserted into the window track or in a hole drilled through the window frame. A duplicate nail on the other side of the window frame increases the safety and causes additional delay for an intruder.

Casement windows are more difficult to break into than double-hung windows, but they are not entry-proof. Casement windows are usually opened with a crank on the inside. If the window is broken, the intruder has only to turn the crank to open the window all the way. Although most casements are rather narrow, a thin man or boy can manage to get into a room without too much difficulty. For protection, remove the crank and place it in a nearby drawer out of reach of an intruder who does not come prepared with a substitute crank for this contingency.

Louvered windows, like casements, are opened with a crank. Breaking them is more difficult and makes more noise, but these too are vulnerable.

Few intruders will break a window. The noise of shattering glass and the difficulty of climbing through sharp glass remnants are strong deterrents. Some thieves, however, tape the glass and use glass cutters. Another technique depends on a fast operation: tape the window, crash, grab and run before police can get there. Impact-resistant or laminated glass can be deterrents against intrusions of this type.

Windows which are not ever likely to be opened can be easily and inexpensively secured. They can be nailed shut or bolted with fixed heavy-gauge screws. A block of wood forced into position and nailed or bolted to the frame will serve to keep most double-hung or casement windows securely closed. A metal grille can be an effective guard against entry through a closed window.

Special Protection for High Risk Locations

Street-level windows and windows facing a fire escape require special security precautions. Iron bars are the most common safety devices, but they should not be installed unless there is adequate provision for exit in case of fire.

Barred windows look safe and will discourage an amateur housebreaker. On the other hand, a professional will use the bars as a fulcrum for prying a window and have little difficulty either pulling them loose or cutting them with a hacksaw.

The chief objection to bars is that they *imprison the householder* in case of a fire or other emergency. The remedy for this is a hinged bar with a lock which, in itself, presents something of an exit problem. Accordion-type grates which can be opened by pulling a lever are the best answer in most cases.

Bars and most types of security measures, such as meshed windows and unbreakable glass, make a home look like a prison. If you must use them, select ornamental grilles or wrought-iron work, which can be obtained for a small additional cost. They add a certain pleasing flavor to the architecture.

Basement Windows

When you check your windows, don't forget to look at basement windows, chutes, ventilation outlets, or other areas which give access to your house, even if you never use them yourself.

Basements are particularly vulnerable areas because they usually are not occupied. Metal basement windows have latches built into them, so that a padlock can be inserted. If a basement window has no lock, drive a screw into the wood or masonry near the edge of the window, leaving enough of the head protruding to stop the window from opening.

Skylights

Skylights should be locked and protected with metal grilles.

A skylight of polycarbonate glass can withstand a ten-pound sledgehammer, but it costs ten times as much as regular glass. Safety glass with a wire mesh is less espensive but not quite as strong. Bars can be placed over the skylight as an alternate type of defense.

Putty

The putty which holds the glass in most windows should be a matter of concern, particularly in an old house. As time passes, putty dries out. Generally, the person who paints your house will replace putty that is cracking away, but some window frames may not have been painted for years, and eventually the plastic material crumbles away, leaving a window loose enough to push out. It is wise to check for this from time to time.

Air Conditioners

Many homes have room air conditioners mounted in window openings. If these are not secured by long, sturdy screws fastened into live (unrotted) wood, the unit may be removed and entry to a home becomes simple. If the cooling unit is not securely fastened, a metal bar, securely anchored to hold the unit, can be an added deterrent.

Plastic Windows

Lexan® windows are as transparent as glass and about the same thickness. They are break-proof and, therefore, offer much more security than ordinary windows. They are widely used. In some places, they are required for storm doors and windows.

Windows That Call for Help!

Obviously, almost any window can be broken. If the door is secure, an intruder will go to a window for what seems to be an easy entry. An experienced thief has learned how to minimize the noise of breaking glass. But there are ways you can equip your windows to "call for help" if an intruder should attempt to enter. A variety of low-cost, easy-to-install alarm systems are now available. More on these in the next chapter.

Chapter 4

Alarms

Alarm systems probably began with a convenient flock of fowl.

The ancient Romans used a gaggle of geese to warn them of intruders. Geese are equally effective today. A truck-equipment company in Paramount, California, uses them to honk an alarm if thieves approach its lot. They are cheap and may even lay eggs!

As we know, there is no lock that will stop a determined, knowledgeable thief. There are good locks and better locks to be sure, but given the time — only a matter of seconds in many cases — and the inclination, plus the expectation of a good haul, a man who makes his living from housebreaking will find a way into your house or office.

Noise Is an Effective Defense

The thing an intruder fears most of all is discovery. A burglar or vandal wants to avoid confrontation. He prefers to work silently, stealthily, at his own pace. A sudden, loud, unexpected alarm blows his cover, throws him into a panic. It threatens to bring investigators, or even the police. It is a rare intruder who will stick around when an alarm is screaming his presence to the world.

> *"Wichita, Kansas — Just a few days after this hardware store installed an <u>Ultrason-X</u> burglar alarm, a would-be thief broke in by way of a hole in the roof. As he walked into the front of the store, he tripped the alarm.*

He was so frightened that he ran down the aisle and right through the plate-glass show window. No one knows how badly he was hurt, but he certainly made a swift exit!"

Today's Breed of Burglar

Few thieves are professionals. They tend to be young people, looking for an easy mark. Half are younger than 18 years old; 90 percent are under 35. They usually are looking for items they can steal easily and sell quickly; radios, TVs, stereos, cameras. But in their search for these things, they are apt to vandalize your home, destroy prized possessions that they can't take, and indulge in incredible acts of malicious mischief.

Given the number of choices of where he can "work," a burglar is less likely to select a home that is reasonably secure. Unless he feels that the valuables you have make the extra risk worthwhile, an alarm system can go a long way toward making him select another target.

Alarm Systems
Need Not Be Expensive

The fundamental purpose of an alarm system is to create noise. Noise will scare off the intruder and will call attention to the fact that something unusual is going on in your home.

Until a few years ago, alarm systems for the home were offshoots of those sold for commercial installations. This made them more elaborate than they needed to be. They required professional installation and often called for a monthly service fee. The net result was that they were far too expensive for the average homeowner.

With more and more families seeking the protection an alarm system can offer, the demand has gradually built a low-cost solution. Several types of systems which the homeowner can easily install himself are now available from locksmiths and hardware departments.

Two Basic Types of Systems — Perimeter and Area Alarms

A **perimeter** alarm system relies on "sensors" mounted on windows and doors. These sensors are commonly two-part magnetic switches . . . one half mounted on the frame, the other on the door or moving part of the window. When the system is armed (turned on) any attempt to open the door or window will separate the two parts of the switch, sounding the alarm.

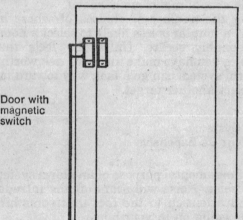

Door with
magnetic
switch

An **area** alarm system consists of a detector placed inside the house in such a way that it protects a specific area and "traps" any intruder who enters it. While there are several types of motion detectors, the most common is the ultrasonic type. These flood a room with inaudible high-frequency sound waves which are reflected off the walls and back to the detector. As long as nothing changes, there is silence. But if an intruder steps into the area covered, the reflected wave pattern changes and the alarm is sounded.

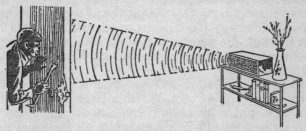

Area alarm sets up "trap zone" which catches an intruder.

Which System is Best for You?

Once you have decided that you want some kind of alarm system, you will want to consider the one or combination that best meets your needs. The aim of the perimeter alarm system is to keep an intruder outside the walls of your home or apartment. If you have a large number of windows and doors to protect, the installation can become expensive. But you can install it a step at a time, starting with your front and back doors, where most break-ins occur. If your situation warrants it, you can add sensors to windows at a later date.

An area protection system requires no installation and offers advantages to the apartment dweller who may not be able to mount sensors on doors and windows. For best results, the detector must be placed so that an intruder will likely pass through the "trap zone," generally a living room or hallway. Many of today's area alarm systems are camouflaged to look like small radios or speakers, so they are not readily noticed or identified by an intruder. The intruder must enter your home to cause such devices to sound an alarm, it is true, but the sudden, unexpected noise of such an alarm usually is sufficient to send a startled thief running — empty-handed.

A combination of both perimeter and area systems might be your best solution if your home poses special problems: possibly perimeter sensors on all doors and windows, plus an internal "trap zone" in case the intruder enters via any hard-to-protect window or entryway. Then, if the trespasser manages to get through the perimeter system without sounding the alarm, the chances are that he'll trip the area "trap" system.

Ease of installation and operation is as important a consideration as cost. Whether professionally installed or put in by a handy homeowner, the system you choose should be dependable, as foolproof as possible, difficult to bypass, and not subject to false alarms or triggering at the wrong time. Since that takes some doing, let's look at examples of each of the systems we have mentioned.

Perimeter Alarm

Least expensive are the do-it-yourself perimeter systems which can be very effective. One advantage is that you can install them piecemeal as time and budget permit, protecting first and foremost your crucial front and back doors. These systems are generally battery-powered for two reasons: safer for do-it-yourself installation and independent of household power in case an intruder cuts power to the home.

Master Lock's Crimefighter Alarm shows how simple yet effective a do-it-yourself system can be. Built-in time delays allow you to enter and leave at will. A powerful electronic siren emits a piercing, pulsating alarm when activated (and mercifully turns itself off after several minutes, thereby preserving the nerves of residents and neighbors). The system also has a personal panic button which can trigger the alarm even when the main system is turned off. The magnetic sensors for doors and windows are easily installed, and additional sensors or sirens can be added at any time. All components are conveniently prewired for simple snap-together installation.

Crimefighter Alarm
permits easy installation
of professional quality components

Any perimeter system should include protection of the most vulnerable doors, windows, and passageways in your home. A careful and thoughtful examination of the property will help determine those points which most need protection. Your budget may have to determine just how far you go in the initial installation. But plan ahead, too, and know what other points you are going to want to protect when you can afford to expand the basic system. Do-it-yourself systems such as Master's Crimefighter Alarm offer additional accessories — sirens, sensors, pressure mats and switches — all prewired and easily added at any time.

Space or Area Alarms

Area alarms for the home generally require no installation and thus are ideal for the apartment dweller. Most common is the ultrasonic motion detector, a compact unit designed to blend inconspicuously with your furnishings. Since the device can be moved from room to room, it is ideal for providing instant protection whenever you want it. Simply plug it into any wall outlet and its ready to protect your home.

Motion detectors sense an intruder's presence by emitting various types of waves and "reading" the bounced-back reflections. Several types are commonly available today.

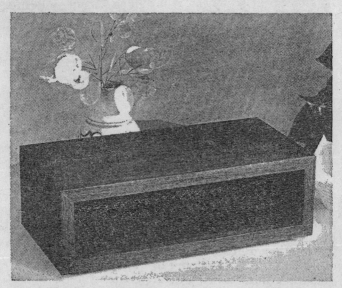

Ultrasonic motion detector blends into surroundings, gives installation-free protection.

Ultrasonic

These motion detectors send out inaudible sound waves and then "read" the pattern of the waves reflected from walls and furnishings. Any intruder interrupts this pattern, causing the alarm to sound. Since a swaying curtain, moths, or a ringing phone can also disturb these reflected waves, one must be careful to purchase a unit with "discriminator" circuitry. This is rarely found in ultrasonic units costing under $150. As a result, cheap units are subject to annoying false alarms. "Discriminator" circuits can distinguish between spurious motion and an actual intruder, making them well worth the additional dollars.

The effective coverage of an ultrasonic unit is stopped by walls, but will generally blanket an area up to 25 or 30 feet long. This makes it ideal for living rooms and hallways — areas that intruders will likely cross.

The Master Lock Ultrason-X unit is a good example of the very sophisticated yet inexpensive systems on the market today. Not only does this unit successfully differentiate between those motions which should and should not trigger the alarm, but it has the added advantage of "satellite" alarm capability. Small, but unobtrusive satellite alarms can be plugged into any electric outlet in your home to relay the warning ... or even installed in the home of a neighbor up to 500 feet away. If an intruder is detected, a simultaneous signal is sent over your household wiring to each satellite, sounding the alarm. Within the trap area, an Ultrason-X can set off "repeaters" at several points, thus surrounding the intruder with a confusion of noise from many directions, making it impossible to spot the actual detector unit. Ultrason-X also permits the addition of magnetic switches to doors or windows to add perimeter protection. Special terminals allow it to be connected to a telephone dialer if you ever wish to tie in with some central station monitoring service.

Optional satellite alarms plug into wall outlets in other rooms or neighbor's house

Microwave or Radar Alarms

These are similar to the ultrasonic systems, except that the extremely short wavelengths are electromagnetic rather than sound. Coverage is somewhat farther than the ultrasonic unit, can be omnidirectional, or can be equipped for aiming in a specific direction. But microwave signals will penetrate walls, so it is necessary to make sure that the installation is adjusted to cover only desired areas to avoid false alarms. Thus professional installation is preferable with microwave systems. These units are not inexpensive, although there is a trend toward lower prices, thanks to solid-state designs.

Infrared Systems

An infrared detector projects a beam of invisible light which is picked up by a receiver. If anyone intrudes and "breaks the beam," the alarm sounds. Often these systems are set up with an arrangement of mirrors which can provide reliable, invisible protection in an intricate pattern throughout a surprisingly large area of your home. If you go this route, you will have to consult a professional installer, as installation requires expert help.

Photoelectric System

Again, this is a "beam of light" system. But since it uses visible light (an "electric eye") it is more easily thwarted than the infrared invisible-beam setup. For this reason, it is less used today than the infrared system. When deployed with properly positioned mirrors, a photoelectric system can provide protection over a long distance. As with infrared, it is costly and generally limited to commercial applications.

Professionally Installed Systems

The obvious advantages of having your system installed for you by a professional are that a specialist can assure you of getting technical equipment properly installed, and that there is no work on your part. However, if you are handy and spend some thoughtful time making your own determinations, the chances are that you can do almost everything a professional can, and about as well. (Exception: if you insist on a telephone-type central-station reporting system, you should definitely engage a professional alarm installer.)

A *local system* makes noise at the house or the apartment where the intrusion is taking place. The noise should accomplish the things we have already noted: scare the intruder away (hopefully empty-handed); warn occupants of the house, if they are home, that a trespasser is around; and alert passersby or neighbors that something unusual is going on where the alarm is sounding. The burglar really has no way of knowing whether or not the system has called the police.

A *central-station alarm system* frequently has as its purpose the apprehension of the intruder. A signal is sent to a local police station or the alarm company's offices, over special leased telephone lines. The signal may be in the form of an automatically dialed prerecorded message or a simple coded signal that alerts the monitors at the central office. The police, fire department, or anyone else can immediately be dispatched to your home.

Although this sounds like an admirable solution, the central alarm system is not without its drawbacks. Many community police departments deplore them, or even refuse to permit them, because of the number of false alarms they have caused. Be sure you check with your local police before you plan to rely on such a system. Also, the signal must be sent over a leased line and there is a monthly service charge for central-station hookup. Moreover, "silent trapping" doesn't stop vandalism, which may be well under way by the time police arrive.

If you elect to have a professionally installed system, be sure that the company you choose to design and install your alarm is reliable. It should be a member of the National Burglar and Fire Alarm Association or have other satisfactory credentials. The parts used should be easily replaceable, and the system should be warranted for at least a year, with a service contract available thereafter. Make sure the estimate includes the total price of all items and labor.

Power for Your Alarm System

The electric power for your system can come either from your regular electrical source or from batteries. If the system is plugged into the standard wiring of the house, it can be rendered inoperative if the wires are cut or if the main switch is turned off. Battery-powered units eliminate this problem. Batteries can be checked through a simple push-button test at the control. Ordinarily, they need be replaced only once a year. There are power packs available which plug into the household electric system and contain back-up battery for power should the regular source of energy fail. Cost is commensurately higher.

Decals — to Use or Not to Use?

Most manufacturers of alarm systems supply warning decals to display on windows and doors. These may deter the amateur by warning him your home is protected. At the same time, this warning removes the element of surprise. If you decide to use decals, make sure they do not indicate the *make* of the system; intruders knowing the make can pretend to be alarm purchasers, and thereby learn how to circumvent your alarm. Avoid the temptation to purchase just decals and not the alarm. Various companies make these available, and they may be quickly identified as phonies by would-be intruders.

To Sum Up

An alarm system is a safe, psychological weapon to protect your life and property. A loud, unexpected noise surprises an intruder, warns him others have been alerted to his presence, and sends him fleeing. Alarm protection need not be expensive and now is available at prices anyone can afford.

The choice of perimeter or area alarms, or a combination of both, is up to you. Your needs and your pocketbook will determine what system is best and affordable for you.

Both do-it-yourself and professionally installed systems can be effective and reliable. Again, the choice is up to you.

For peace of mind, for the protection of your valuables, for the protection of your family, you owe it to yourself to make certain that your home is as burglar-proof as possible, through the use of proper locks plus the back-up protection an alarm system can give.

Chapter 5

When You Are Inside the House

Your home is your castle. You feel safe inside. You should, but you should also realize that for many thieves an occupied house is no deterrent, and, for some, it is even a challenge.

> *"Four Rob Card Party: Guest Is Raped"*
>
> *"A quiet card party among six friends, most of them elderly, ended violently in a Northwest apartment Wednesday night when four intruders robbed the players, raped a 52-year-old woman and shot a 69-year-old man in the jaw.*
>
> *"Police said three male intruders who rushed into the first floor apartment at 1806 T St. behind a woman in her 20's netted $357.20 in the robbery."*
>
> — Washington Post

Safety First with Strangers at the Door

Obviously, the first rule for safety at home is "never let a stranger in" and make sure the person at the door is identifiable in some fashion.

Unless you know the person and feel safe with him or her, you do not have to open the door, and you should not, unless you have been satisfied by some form of identification. Use a peephole to inspect strangers. A uniform and even printed forms are not always sufficient. Almost anyone can rent the uniform of a police officer, maintenance man or a mailman at a costume house. Printed forms can be stolen and duplicated. You must use considerable discretion at this point. Ask them to slip credentials under the door. If you wish to check, don't hesitate to call the office from which the person at the door is supposed to have come. If it appears that the card is not authentic, call the police and stall: "I am getting dressed."

If an unfamiliar delivery man says he has a package for you, ask him to leave it on the porch, and pick it up later, after he has gone. If he says you must sign for the package, demand some identification before you open the door. Judge the situation carefully. Start by asking yourself if you are *expecting* a package.

If you advertise for a lost pet, to sell a car, or to have a garage sale, try to make sure the caller is a person you want to see before you open the door. If you go out, of course, lock the door behind you to insure the individual or a confederate does not gain entry. The caller may simply be trying to get you out of the house.

Here are two other tips to help meet strangers safely at your front door. A convex mirror placed opposite your peephole viewer provides a reflection of anyone else waiting nearby. A favorite ploy of thieves is to have a young person ring your bell while a bigger male thief stands just out of view, ready to force his way in should you open your door. If your home has an alarm system, it is easy to mount a panic button next to the door. Then, if you must open your door, and find a would-be intruder, you can send him fleeing at the touch of a button.

Intercom System

An intercom system can be a valuable, but not necessarily expensive, surveillance tool. Indoor/outdoor units should be fitted at each exterior door, enabling you to ask, "Who is it and what do you want?" before you open the door. Installation of such a unit is relatively simple, very speedy, and quite effective. If you are moving into a new home, you may want to consider having a much more efficient multiple-station intercom unit installed throughout the house. With such a system, a stranger at the door can be checked from any room in the house (even from the bathroom, in case you get caught there). You can also arrange for individual intercom units in the garage or in other areas for nighttime monitoring.

Looking in from Outside

Valuable works of art or antiques should be shielded from view from an outside window whenever practical. The person who sees something he would like to have or could sell is tempted. Temptation can be a first step toward a crime.

Telephone Tactics

A not-uncommon ploy in the suburbs and rural areas is the call for help. "May I use your phone? My car broke down." "I'm lost. Could I call someone for directions?" "My child is sick. Can I call my doctor?" The best response is to ask for the name or phone number and offer to make the call yourself.

As in most things, common sense and a healthy dose of caution will help protect you in your dealings with strangers at the door or on the phone. Do not tell a stranger that your neighbor is away or anything else about the neighborhood that might possibly be useful to outsiders. Do not tell anyone that you are alone in the house or volunteer the information that a member of the household is not expected until such-and-such a time.

It is a good idea **NOT** to display your name on

your mailbox or front door. It is too easy for a thief to look up your phone number in the directory and call ahead to see if anyone is at home.

Your Keys

Your keys need special protection both at home and outside. Do not leave them on a table or desk or even loose in your coat pocket when you check your coat or hang it on a rack.

In the course of time, many people come into your house: delivery men, a cleaning woman, baby sitters, meter men, the plumber, the man from the diaper service. Assuming 99 percent are honest, the other 1 percent may pick up your keys, take them, even for a few minutes, to take an impression from them, and use them to gain entry later. Such people are likely to know when you plan to be away, even for a few hours. If you must trust someone, do not do it carelessly.

If you lose your keys, consider having the cylinders of your locks changed. Do not hope that the keys will turn up. If your keys are out of your possession for even a few hours, you should assume that they have been copied.

Losing keys or having them duplicated offers an extra hazard to a householder. Many, if not most, insurance companies require proof of forced entry to make the policy effective. If a thief enters with keys, the protection of the insurance policy may be lost.

Some people are optimists. They attach a tag to their key rings: Please return to Jane Doe, 5 Some Street, Anywhere, State. It is, of course, possible that a thief will leave them on the kitchen counter . . . after he has emptied the rest of your apartment or home!

Do not hide keys. A thief knows all the places of which you would normally think.

If you drive a car and have occasion to park it in a public lot or a garage with the key in the motor ignition, make sure you remove all keys except the one that turns on the ignition. It is not unheard of for dishonest people to work in a parking lot. It takes only a few minutes to duplicate a key or even to take a wax impression from which a key can be made.

A Dog?

Unquestionably, a dog in the house or in the yard deters an intruder. Whether you have a small dog with a loud bark or a large intimidating animal, a dog becomes an added risk factor for a thief. If you are at home, a dog's sensitive smell and hearing can give you extra warning time.

Dogs are fine for watching. They bark. They can be taught to attack an intruder, but there are many things they cannot be taught, such as to distinguish between an intruder and your neighbor's five-year-old child or your visiting aunt. They generally will not refuse any kind of food; a thief can offer poisoned or doped food to put them out of action.

Bear in mind, the dog is not infallible. Many burglars have a way with animals, and others are not averse to harming one.

Attack Dogs

An attack dog can be any large animal trained to be aggressive toward strangers and very protective of family members. Because such dogs can be terribly vicious, they can sometimes generate more problems than they solve. One incident of severe aggression against an innocent party could conceivably involve the owner in a lawsuit that could be ruinous. Rather than an attack dog, choose a dog that can create a lot of noise. Noise that will scare away an intruder is what you really want from a watchdog.

A Gun in the House

Should you keep a gun in the house?

"No!" Unless you know well how to use one, can practice with it on a regular basis, and know the laws (and obey them) concerning possession of a deadly weapon.

For people who know how to handle a gun and how to handle themselves, a gun can be good protection. For others, it can be the means to a shortened life. Bear in mind that many of the murders which take place in the United States involve relatives and friends shooting each other in the heat of a dispute. Most murderers know their victims because they are a brother or a wife, a close friend or a husband. It is necessary, therefore, to honestly assess your own ability to act responsibly.

A gun offers several alternatives to a thief. He can (1) shoot first, (2) try to take the gun away from you by stealth or force, or (3) run. In many instances, a gun becomes a threat to the owner reluctant to use it.

Think about this possible scenario. You are awakened from a deep sleep by the sound of an intruder in your room. In your sleepy state you reach over and begin fumbling for the gun you have carefully placed by your bed. The intruder, being wide awake, realizes what you're after. He moves swiftly to the night table and grabs the gun before you are able to take it out of the drawer. Now, instead of facing a situation where an intruder, on waking you, has stealthily sneaked out of the room, you are looking down the barrel of your gun in the hands of that intruder. It is a situation fraught with danger for both of you.

Guns also enhance the possibility of accidentally injuring or killing people who get their hands on them. This is particularly true of children. Many an "unloaded" gun has killed the unwary.

If you are especially vulnerable, carry a good deal of cash, are adept at using and caring for a weapon, it is tempting to be able to protect yourself. But be sure to check the laws of your state to determine the licensing requirements for carrying a concealed weapon.

If you do have a gun in the house, make sure that every adult in your family knows how to use the weapon and that children do not have access to it. Remember that a weapon in your hand may tempt a thief to use any weapon he has, and he is under even greater tension than you are.

The sight of a weapon adds a whole new dimension of violence and adds considerably to the chance that someone may be hurt in a robbery. It can be argued, however, that if you have a weapon — even if you fire a warning shot over the victim — it may save your life where violence is part of the thief's plan and intention.

Most important, if you have a gun, be sure it is locked up so it won't be stolen, cannot be useful to an intruder who may get to it first, or dangerous to a careless child or visitor who picks it up out of curiosity.

Emergency Equipment

Every house and apartment should have (1) a flashlight, (2) replacement batteries, (3) fire extinguishers, and (4) a transistor radio in case of a power failure. A supply of canned foodstuffs is also a wise precaution.

Each telephone instrument should have at least these three emergency phone numbers displayed: the police, the fire department, and the nearest hospital. Never mind that you may have memorized them. Tension steals one's memory in a crisis and you do not want to have to grope for a number in an emergency.

However, this does not mean you should not learn the local police number. If you can't think of it (and 911 is not operative in your area), dial O for the operator and ask her to connect you. In addition, there should be a list of other numbers you might need to call in an emergency.

If You Are in a House When a Thief Enters

If you are in bed, lie quietly, as if you were asleep. Try to avoid a confrontation. A burglar may react violently when he is surprised, so he can get out quickly. As soon as you can safely do so, call the police.

If you walk in on an intruder, walk out and call for help. If a panic button is at the door, set it off.

Try to have the cool of one couple who walked into their home, saw some burglars at work and said, "Sorry, we must be in the wrong house." They departed and called the police from a neighbor's home. Quick thinking and a calm approach gave them the edge.

Making Your Property Unique

One factor that is very important to a thief is an ability to turn stolen property into cash quickly for enough money to make his theft worth the time and risk. If you mark your property so that it is specifically, uniquely yours, the property becomes less marketable. It can be identified as (1) stolen, and (2) yours if it is recovered.

A small etching tool is available to engrave your name or a special identifying number on television sets, stereo equipment, radios, cameras, binoculars, typewriters, anything of metal that has substantial resale value. Some police departments have these for loan. Police advise using your driver's license number so that if anything is stolen, it can be identified and returned to you.

As a deterrent, decals are provided to advise a prospective thief that equipment has been marked.

Hopefully, this will discourage entry and especially the theft of these items which are often the most marketable in your home. Commonly referred to as "Operation Identification," this system was begun in 1963 by Police Chief Everett F. Halloday and, in less than two decades, has spread throughout the nation.

There is a national identification and registration organization which will supply you with a number. Listfax Corporation has set up a computerized system called "Identifax" that puts your personally-assigned number into a nationwide registration. For additional information, contact Identifax Nationwide Registry, 600 Third Avenue, New York, NY 10016.

Hiding Place

No place you can think of to hide your valuables has not been used before, whether it is in the refrigerator or under a pile of vegetables.

However, most thieves don't risk a full search. They want to get in and out. So hiding things is the next best thing to putting items in a locked place which, after all, can't be totally burglar-proof.

The best hiding places are built-ins which look like something else or like nothing at all: a hat rack, fake

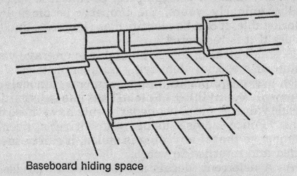

Baseboard hiding space

or real, that hinges off to a hiding place; a hole in the wall; a door that looks like an air conditioning vent; a false bottom on a bookshelf; a hole behind an actual but hinged baseboard; a dummy electrical outlet; a false floor; a space behind a shelf of glassware; a false-bottomed drawer.

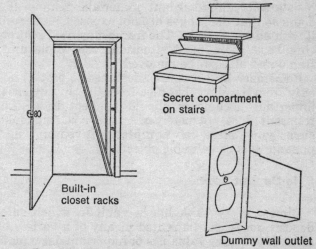

Secret compartment on stairs

Built-in closet racks

Dummy wall outlet

A Safe at Home

A safe in your home has many advantages and it need not be expensive. Some built-in desk-cabinet-safes fit into a closet and form a handy office when the door is opened. A safe is not burglar-proof against a determined thief, but it protects against fire and against thieves who are unskilled or too much in a hurry to assault the defense a safe offers. Moreover, the whole thing is not too obvious if it is enclosed.

A small wall safe, particularly if it can be concealed, offers more protection. The choice depends on the extent of your valuables and your budget. The floor safe, although it may weigh several hundred pounds, is also portable and can be removed if the burglar can't open it with a chisel or torch. It is a good idea to remove the wheels and bolt the safe to the floor. A good safe should be capable of resisting a torch and other tools for at least thirty minutes.

Another solution is to select a closet which is not too necessary for everyday use, line it with fire-resistant or fire-retardant materials, rehang the doors so that the hinges are not exposed, and equip it with adequate locks. The frame may need reinforcing because in most situations the whole unit, frame and all, can be removed.

Remember that a safe is designed to protect not only from burglary, but also from fire. In any case, important documents should be kept in a fire-resistant place, not merely in a metal box. And make sure you have a complete inventory and photographs of valuable objects.

Safe-Deposit Boxes

Almost every bank has a vault in which safe-deposit boxes can be rented in any of a variety of sizes. If you have valuables or important documents which you do not need to use often, they should be in such a box. The loss of even registered bonds and stocks can be an expensive experience. Valuable jewelry, even if you wear it quite often and it is insured, should be kept in such a vault.

Although it is the safest place available, a safe-deposit box does not offer the 100 percent security most people think it does. Vaults have been entered and robbed with much notoriety in recent years. Vault insurance is available for a small fee. If all your life savings are in a safe-deposit box, you might give some thought to this, especially if your securities are negotiable.

Securities

It is always wise to have stocks and bonds

registered in your name so that they are not negotiable without your signature. Many tax-exempt municipal bonds cannot be registered in "name of owner" and are issued "to bearer" instead. Each bond is numbered and you should keep a list of these in a place apart from where the bonds are kept. Freely negotiable instruments such as these are almost like cash and should be kept by a bank or with a broker. If these certificates are stolen and you have to replace them, the process is both time-consuming and costly. Corporations will require that a bond be posted in case another claim is made. The cost may be 5 percent of the value of the securities.

If your broker holds certificates for you, the federal government insures these, but there have been instances where brokerage houses have been robbed and a bankruptcy results in long delays in recovering customers' securities.

If you want to sell a stock or bond that has been stolen, even greater complications result. It may be months before a replacement certificate is available to you.

Of what use is the certificate to a thief? Organized crime figures use stolen certificates for collateral on loans by forging any signature required. Until the loans are due and called, which may be years later, the lender does not know that the collateral is stolen and worthless.

Chapter 6

Especially for Apartment Dwellers

Ideally, an apartment house should have a twenty-four hour doorman service. Every visitor who enters the building should be identified by a tenant. Elevators should be attended. Doors to the stairways should open only from the hallways except at roof and lobby levels, where they should be open only from the stairwells. Doors to the garages should be self-closing and, preferably, attended.

Unfortunately, the ideal is always expensive and frequently impractical. There are practical substitutes which the landlord can supply, however, and there are steps which you as an individual apartment dweller can take to make your life safer and more secure.

An intercom system, preferably one combined

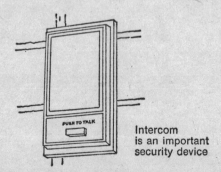

Intercom
is an important
security device

with a closed-circuit television system, can go a long way toward keeping unauthorized people out of the building. Any tenant would be able to know precisely who is asking to come in before pressing the buzzer which opens the lobby door.

Your apartment can be safe, safer even than a house with several ground-level entrances. But it, too, requires safeguards on windows and doors, especially windows accessible by way of a fire escape or ledge or terrace.

The outside and the hallways of an apartment building should be sufficiently lighted so that you can read a newspaper's headlines. Shrubbery should be trimmed to provide minimum cover for a person at an entranceway.

When You Move In

When you move in, change the locks. See that a peephole viewer and a chain lock are installed.

Doors to the garage should be controlled by a key or a magnetic card. They should close automatically and the keys should be changed once a year.

Lighting should be adequate, with protective fixtures that make removing the bulb more difficult.

Mirrors at the bends in the hallway and outside peepholes should make hiding impossible.

Proper maintenance of doors, lights, and firefighting equipment should not be left to the discretion of a "super" or landlord. If you see that something is amiss, know that it is as important as life or death, and see that something is done about it.

Do not hide a key. Even if it is there when you look for it, you will never know if someone has made a copy.

Do Not Leave Your Door Unlocked — Ever

It is a temptation to leave the door to your apartment ajar or closed but unlocked when you're just stepping out for a minute. Even if you are just taking out the garbage, or picking up your mail, or moving the car, or chatting with a neighbor on the next floor — *lock your door*. It takes an extra few seconds to make sure you have your keys with you, and it seems like a nuisance to have to unlock your door when you return. But at least you can be pretty certain that no intruder will use the moment you are out to sneak in and await your return.

The "Super's" Keys

Many buildings require that the superintendent have a key to provide access to your apartment in case of a flood, fire, or other emergency. This involves several hazards. "Supers" change. "Supers" get robbed. (There go all the keys to all the apartments.)

Some alternatives include leaving a key in a sealed envelope with a neighbor. If you must leave a key with the "super," put it in a sealed envelope. Cover the flap with clear tape and sign across the tape to prevent unauthorized opening. Ask to see the envelope from time to time.

Windows

Special gates are available for fire escape windows. They *must* be easily opened from the inside and not at all from the outside. A folding accordion-type with a lever that can be quickly opened in an emergency is best. Don't put bars on fire escape windows; they can cost you your life. As an alternative, a break-proof glass window is available.

Your Neighbors

Knowing your neighbors, and being friendly with them, is an especially important safety factor for apartment dwellers. Caring will help you to be alert for each other, and for everyone else in the building. It may be gossip, but comparing notes about strangers, suspicious incidents, and malfunctioning of equipment can all provide important precautionary information.

Area Alarm and Satellite Stations

A portable area alarm, like Master Lock's Ultrason-X unit, makes it possible for one or more neighbors to know immediately if there is an intruder in your apartment. Inexpensive, unobtrusive satellite alarms which plug into a regular electric outlet in any of several nearby apartments will sound a warning if the basic system in your apartment indicates the presence of anyone who should not be there. The neighbor(s) can then easily call the police and notify the superintendent. See chapter 4 for a complete description of this system.

Elevators

Elevators can be a hazard. Self-service elevators in buildings where there are no guards can be especially dangerous. A few basic precautions might literally mean the difference between life and death.

Do not enter an elevator if there is a stranger or a suspicious-looking person who makes you nervous. **Do** wait for the empty elevator to come back for you.

Do not ride an elevator down to the basement if you are headed up. **Do** wait for the car to come back to the lobby where you can make sure the elevator is safe before you enter it.

Do not go to the laundry room or basement alone. **Do** make sure that a neighbor or friend goes with you, for the protection of both of you.

Do hold the door open when you press the button for your floor. If the arrow indicates you will go up, release the door. If the arrow points down, get out! It could mean that someone has called the elevator to the basement, hoping to bring you with it. Wait for the car to return to the lobby and inspect it before you get in to go up to your floor.

Do move around to the panel so that you can be ready to press the alarm button should anyone in the elevator with you arouse your suspicions or annoy you.

Do carry your key in your hand so you don't have to search for it while you're in the elevator or standing in front of your apartment door.

Do not spend the time to empty your mailbox or stay in the lobby late at night if you are alone. Go up to your apartment right away and pick up the mail in the morning.

Be sure to report any elevator problems to the superintendent or the landlord. If the gates or doors are not working properly, they should be repaired. If the hatch in the ceiling of the elevator is loose or open, have someone investigate.

Laundry Rooms

Laundry rooms are often lonely places and often dangerous ones. Try to arrange to do your laundry with a neighbor. If you are alone, be alert. If you see something unusual, or hear suspicious noises, get out quickly.

Your Mailbox

*"Two Convicted in Fraud
of Stolen Welfare Checks"*

"The former president of a now-defunct Federal credit union and the self-styled pastor of a Brownsville church were convicted in Federal District Court in Brooklyn Friday on charges of conspiring to buy and

cash more than $190,000 in stolen Federal and city welfare checks."

The checks you receive are a year-round temptation to not so petty thieves who make their living out of mailboxes — other people's mailboxes.

These checks pass through many hands in the process of being written, mailed, and delivered. One of the first things you should do is make a list of the checks due each month and check them off when you deposit or cash them. As soon as you get a check, mark it "for deposit only" if you are not going to cash it. This prevents its being cashed if you lose it. Do not sign it until you are ready to cash it.

One of the most vulnerable spots in the whole line of earnings-to-spending is your mailbox. A screwdriver can open almost any mailbox, but thieves make it a point to get an easily obtainable passkey. A thief has little difficulty in spending, cashing, or selling a small check.

If a check is overdue on your schedule, check with the sender. If two or three days have passed since the time a check should have arrived and you have not received it, ask that it be stopped and a new one issued.

In general, you are not responsible for a check that does not carry your endorsement. The person who cashes it does so at his own risk. But getting a check replaced can be a trying nuisance.

Some buildings have a mailbox patrol to watch for the postman, especially during the first five days of the month and during the 15th-through-the-20th period.

If you go away for a few days or more, ask a neighbor to empty your mailbox. If you have delivery through a mail slot in your door, arrange to have any packages left outside picked up. The best solution is to arrange to have checks mailed directly to your bank and deposited by the bank to your account.

Mail that piles up, no matter where you live, is a dead tip-off to a thief that you are not at home. If you go away for a two-week, or even a one-week, vacation you can make arrangements with your local post office to hold your mail for you to be picked up on your return. Or, as noted, have a neighbor pick up your mail and any packages for you.

Chapter 7

Protection of Property Outside the House

"$350 Prize Bike Swiped by Thieves"

"It was ten speed. It was shiny new. It was valued at $350. And it was the pride of 13-year-old Dane Allen, who received it last week as winner of the 'Newsboy Sales Booster Award of the Year.' Dane's prize vanished from the driveway of his home yesterday when he left it unlocked during the few moments it took to eat lunch before leaving to meet a friend. Neighbors reported seeing a youngster riding the bike around the time of its disappearance. They 'thought it was a school friend giving his new bike a try.' No trace of Dane's prize has been seen since.

"The loss again prompted authorities to urge parents to warn youngsters they should always lock their bikes securely to a tree, post or other solid tethering point, even when leaving the bike for brief intervals. Few stolen bikes, they state, ever find their way back to their owners, although thousands are lost this way every year."

The threat to your security obviously extends beyond the walls of your home. Garages, sheds, boathouses, bicycles, and other targets for thieves must be adequately locked. For most situations, this means the right choice of padlocks, hasps, security chains, and cables.

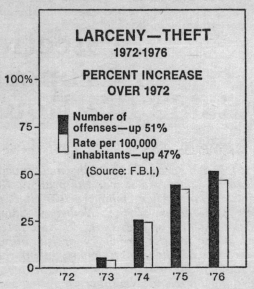

Like door locks, padlocks come in all degrees of security, from simple nuisance protection to strong deterrence. Knowing what to look for is important in buying a padlock, since certain recognizable features add to the security — and the cost — of the lock you select.

While no device can give absolute protection, the right padlock presents a great impediment to thieves. Most thieves do not have the knowledge, determination, or tools to break a good lock. Nor do they have the time or patience. So select a padlock geared to the value of the property to be safeguarded. Its cost is slight compared to most other security hardware.

How to Choose a Padlock

What are the real keys to security when you select a padlock? Here are important features you should look for:

1. A laminated or extruded case; the thicker the better, to resist pounding or smashing.
2. Case-hardened steel shackle. Alloy steels can add even more resistance to cutting. And with shackles too — the thicker the better.
3. A double-locking shackle, to double resistance to attempts at prying the shackle out of the case.
4. Precision pin-tumbler locking mechanism.
5. Corrosion protection against moisture and weather.

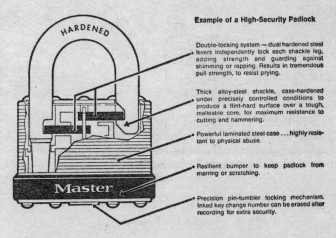

Example of a High-Security Padlock

HARDENED

Double-locking system — dual hardened steel levers independently lock each shackle leg, adding strength and guarding against shimming or rapping. Results in tremendous pull strength, to resist prying.

Thick alloy-steel shackle, case-hardened under precisely controlled conditions to produce a flint-hard surface over a tough, malleable core, for maximum resistance to cutting and hammering.

Powerful laminated steel case ... highly resistant to physical abuse.

Resilient bumper to keep padlock from marring or scratching.

Precision pin-tumbler locking mechanism. Inked key change number can be erased after recording for extra security.

Master

When in doubt about hidden qualities such as the construction of the inner locking mechanism, the manufacturer's track record can be used as a fair guide. An example is the largest maker of padlocks in the United States — Master Lock Company of Milwaukee, Wisconsin. They manufacture over thirty million locks a year, and are considered the standard of protection by locksmiths, industrial users, schools and institutions, and others. Their line includes more than one hundred varieties, some for very specialized security problems and some to meet the most common problems. Generations of youngsters have had as their first personal padlock

the very familiar Master® combination lock used on
their school locker or bike.

Wrought-Steel Padlocks — Nuisance Protection

Wrought-steel or "shell" padlocks are the lowest
priced locks you can buy. They are a good investment if you understand that they are intended main-
ly for nuisance protection, such as keeping the kids
out of your toolbox, locking power tools against

Shell padlock

tampering, restricting access to a mailbox,
storeroom, or cage, for example. They cost little and
they can prevent thoughtless misadventures or injury from hazardous household or industrial items.

Laminated Steel Padlocks — A Security Breakthrough

One nagging problem in making a burglar-
deterrent lock lies in protecting the lock mechanism.
For centuries, locks had hollow cases, and a crowbar
or a hammer blow could often shatter this "shell,"
loosen the lock mechanism, and thus destroy the
protective value of the padlock.

Then, about fifty years ago, a locksmith named
Harry Soref set out to create a lock that could not be
easily opened by smashing. Taking a whole new approach, he designed a tremendously powerful
padlock in which the case was built up out of
laminated steel plates. From each plate he removed

just enough metal to accommodate the part of the locking mechanism passing through it. These plates were then stacked to form the laminated padlock case, and riveted together under thousands of pounds of pressure, forming a case stronger than a solid block of steel.

The enormous strength of this approach is easily demonstrated with a telephone book or a piece of plywood. Page by page, a telephone book can be ripped to shreds. But closed it cannot be torn. The same holds true in comparing the strength of plywood with that of a similar-size pine board.

Even Soref's earliest laminated padlocks, fashioned from pieces of scrap metal with hand tools, were able to withstand powerful sledgehammer blows and show little more than a surface dent.

This was the first application of the now familiar principle of lamination applied to a common household item. Since then, lamination has provided the key to greatly strengthening many products, ranging from furniture to the basic materials used in building our homes.

Warded Locks

The "warded" type of padlock is easily recognized by its straight key with simple matching notches cut

Warded padlock

into both edges. These locks give low-cost pilfer protection at a price slightly higher than shell locks but less than pin-tumbler high-security padlocks. They are important where property is of significant but limited value, and are intended for securing such items as oil-tank caps, well covers, beach lockers, duffel bags, or barn doors.

Because they offer relatively large clearances between internal moving parts, warded locks are frequently preferred under conditions where sand, water, ice, or other contaminants are a problem.

However, a word of caution: a laminated warded padlock may look almost identical to a pin-tumbler padlock at first glance, and this is a potential pitfall for lock users. There is a decided difference in security between these two mechanisms. Since a warded padlock may cost as little as half the price of a pin-tumbler padlock while outwardly looking similar, many uninformed consumers make a wrong buying decision where high security is required.

Pin-Tumbler Locks

Controlled by finely machined precision mechanisms, this type of padlock offers premium

Pin-tumbler padlock

protection and thousands of key selections that guard against accidental duplication. Compared to a warded mechanism with only a few working elements, a similar appearing four-pin-tumbler lock will have 19 or more precision parts contributing to maximum security. Look for a double-locking shackle too, with independent locking of each shackle leg. The result is a padlock extremely difficult to open by picking, forcing, shimming, or rapping, and which provides extra resistance to saws and bolt cutters.

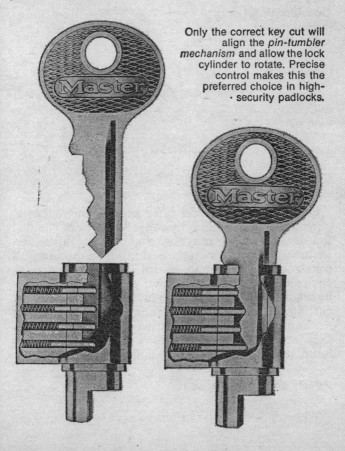

Only the correct key cut will align the *pin-tumbler mechanism* and allow the lock cylinder to rotate. Precise control makes this the preferred choice in high-security padlocks.

Hardened Shackles

For added security, look for the legend "hardened" on the lock shackle, and the words "case hardened" on padlock packaging. This means the steel has been specially heat-treated to provide an extra-hard outer layer resistant to cutting and sawing, with a tough inner core so the shackle won't be brittle and easy to break. On the finest locks, special alloy steels add to the toughness of the shackles.

Combination Locks

With a combination padlock there is no key to lose.

Combination padlocks offer keyless convenience, particularly valuable for youngsters, where you feel the loss of keys may be a problem. Protection features to look for include reinforced double-wall construction — tough stainless-steel outer case enclosing a sturdy steel inner case — plus a case-hardened steel shackle for added resistance against cutting and sawing. Combination locks are rated as medium security. Do not settle for a cheap combination lock. Better quality locks are more resistant to force, prying, and manipulation.

Power against Corrosion

Where you face conditions of severe corrosion, as

along seacoasts, aboard boats, near refineries, and in areas of high humidity and atmospheric pollution, you may find it preferable to invest in hard-wrought-brass versions of high-security laminated padlocks, which are available expressly for such situations. For maximum protection against corrosion, the shackle typically will be chrome- or nickel-plated hardened steel, and most inner parts will be constructed of brass, stainless steel or nickel-plated steel. But for extreme environmental conditions, even the shackle can be brass if preferred. You can expect the price of a maximum-security brass padlock to run substantially higher than that of its steel counterpart.

Solid brass padlocks protect against the elements.

A lower cost medium-security alternative for the average user is the solid-brass padlock. Again, look for pin-tumbler locking and a case-hardened shackle to protect valuable property. These locks cost substantially less than heavy-duty laminated brass padlocks, and are particularly useful for many coastal area uses, as with boats, outdoor lockers, gates, and so forth.

Choosing a Hasp

Hasps can be the weak link in the security chain. When locking garage doors, sheds, boathouses, warehouses, or other enclosures, by means of a hasp, your padlock is in fact only as strong as the hasp on which it is hung. Use only a strong, weather-resistant hasp with concealed screws. A rust-prone hasp may allow rust to drip down through the shackle opening of the padlock and "freeze" the mechanism.

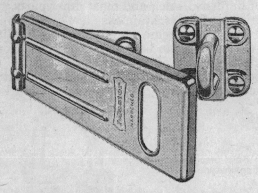

Choose a well-made hasp for worry-free protection.

For full protection your hasp should be case-hardened steel to resist a bolt cutter or hacksaw. Mounting screws should be concealed when the hasp is in the closed position, to prevent tampering. For the same reason, a pinless hinge design gives additional strength and protection needed to resist rip-off artists.

When mounting the hasp, make certain it is securely screwed into live wood at least as thick as the screws are long. For extra protection, bolt it in place if you can. And, speaking of possible weak links — make sure that the hasp "eye" that holds the lock is as thick in diameter as the padlock used with it.

The Hasp Lock — Unitized Protection

There are places where padlocks "wander away"

from hasps if left unlocked — they may be misplaced or stolen. One excellent solution to this common problem is a device that evolved out of the hasp, known as the hasp lock. Here the hasp and lock are one — a unit. The action of the hasp lock is like that

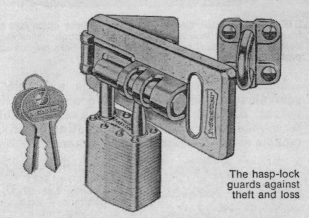

The hasp-lock
guards against
theft and loss

of the dead-bolt door lock. A sliding bolt with permanently attached padlock mechanism engages the locking "eye." Look for the same quality features recommended for the hasp: hardened steel, weather resistance, and so forth.

Choosing Chains and Cables

Chains and cables can extend the security of padlocking to a wide variety of movable and mobile possessions. Bicycles, lawn and garden equipment, boats, motorcycles can be tethered to a post, tree, dock, or other immovable object.

Common chain available in hardware stores does not offer high security. Buy the kind specifically designed for locking applications. Be sure it is case hardened for high resistance to cutters, saws, and files. Individual links should be welded, not just twisted, to resist being pried apart.

STRONGER THREE WAYS — Rugged security chain has case-hardened steel surface to resist cutting, and tough malleable steel core to guard against breaking. Welded steel links provide strong protection against prying.

Multi-stranded security cable is available for equivalent protection, with the added benefit of light weight. Examine cable closely, as some manufacturers add a thicker than usual coating of vinyl to make a small steel strand look bigger.

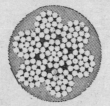

THE STRENGTH OF INTERTWINED STEEL! Cable consists of seven individual strands — each containing 19 separate steel wires — intertwined to make cutting more difficult.

In general, the thicker the chain or cable, the greater the protection. Take care to match the strength of the padlock to the chain or cable. And position the lock and cable (or chain) as high off the ground as possible. This makes it difficult for thieves to gain extra leverage by bracing one leg of a bolt cutter against the ground.

Care Pays Off

Unlike many products today, a well-made padlock asks little care and gives many years of dependable service. Do your locks a favor, though, and occasionally oil the keyway and the shackle openings. (But don't overdo a good thing — too much oil can be bad news, gumming up any precision mechanism.)

In corrosive environments, padlocks should be lubricated on a regular schedule. Occasionally, they should be dipped in kerosene and re-oiled to assure long life and trouble-free operation.

Many fine padlocks come with their key number stamped in ink on the bottom of the body. Record this number in a safe place. If you lose your keys, that number will help you get a duplicate key from your store, your locksmith, or the manufacturer. But be sure to erase the inked number from the lock so would-be thieves cannot use it to get a duplicate key.

When in Doubt about a Lock

Ask your local police department for advice. Many have experts to help you, and may have displays of security padlocks as well as related locks for special purposes (gun locks, ski locks, outboard motor locks, etc.).

If you are in doubt about a choice of padlock and cannot get expert advice, here are some useful guidelines: (1) buy the best padlock protection you can afford (strength and cost generally coincide); (2) when possible avoid leaving locked items in out-of-the-way places where thieves have time to work on the lock unseen; (3) if locked property is of a nature that has strong appeal to the light-fingered, and has substantial value, back up your locks with some insurance.

Chapter 8

Helpful Tips for Hard-to-lock Property

It is an all too familiar scenario, punctuated by an explosive, heartbreaking "accident."

"Boy, 4, Is Killed Playing with Gun"

"A four-year-old Memphis boy was fatally shot by his seven-year-old sister Sunday afternoon as they played with a gun the boy found in their home.

"Thomas Brecklin died in the basement of his home at 1860 E. Orchid Road. A bullet from his mother's 25-caliber automatic struck him in the chest and went through his body.

"His mother, Terri, 31, told police she had taken the gun from the top of the refrigerator while cleaning and had removed the bullet clip before placing the gun on a kitchen chair.

"But Sgt. Michael Wolf of the police homicide division said she had not removed the bullet from the gun chamber.

"Mrs. Brecklin said she did not notice Thomas pick up the gun and take it downstairs where his sister and a six-year-old brother were playing.

"Police said Thomas gave the gun to his sister, who pointed it at him and pulled the trigger."

The tragedy of the "unloaded gun" is played out at the expense of death or injury to more than twenty-three thousand children and adults each year. About 60 percent of these accidents occur *in the victim's home*. That says something of major importance to owners of firearms.

Curiosity kills . . . the *gun lock* can be a major lifesaver.

Guns and certain specialized sports and outdoor equipment present unique security problems. Frequently it is not desirable or practical to keep such property under storeroom lock and key. Yet conventional padlocks may not be well adapted to the valuables you wish to protect.

The danger of guns in the home being stolen or mishandled is a major case in point. Inevitably, specialized needs like this have spawned a breed of locking devices quite distinct from padlocks. We shall examine some basic examples here.

All these locks are readily available from hardware stores, locksmiths, sporting-goods dealers, and department stores.

Gun Lock — Guards Life as Well as Property

Several styles of gun locks are available. The inexpensive, attractive lock illustrated can be used on nearly all firearms. The method of locking makes it a lifesaver as well as a theft thwarter. It completely blocks access to the trigger, rendering the gun useless to thieves.

As with high-security padlocks, the locking mechanism uses a precision pin-tumbler cylinder. Keyed-alike gun locks can be obtained, giving access to all firearms in a collection with a single key.

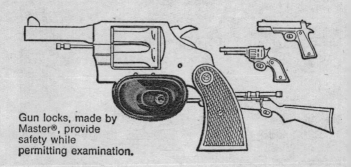

Gun locks, made by Master®, provide safety while permitting examination.

This style of gun lock allows you to display a prized firearm on an open gun rack. While people are free to examine the gun, the lock prevents dry-firing and protects the firing pin, as well as insuring against "unloaded gun" misadventures.

Campers Offer Thieves Easy Pickings

The highly popular outdoor recreational vehicle raises a wide range of security challenges. First, there's the costly and vulnerable camper itself, hard to trace when stolen, easily snatched by thieves, with a huge market of eager buyers awaiting a deal. Then there are the contents, often of considerable worth. Stereos, cameras, radios, fishing gear, stove, refrigerator, and so on, are common, depending on your personal interests and family activities.

The camper itself, however, is the big plum thieves are after. And you would be surprised how swiftly they can make off with one. The door locks can quickly be defeated by knowledgeable criminals. They will have it open, hot-wired and rolling in little more time than it might take you to get it unlocked and started using the keys. (For some helpful tips on beefing up motor vehicle security so thieves pass you over in favor of an easier mark, see the chapter on Auto Security.)

The protection of your camper calls for making things as tough as possible for thieves. When it is not in use, keep it in a secure place next to or behind your home. Or rent space in some high-security, fenced-in storage facility, available in most towns and cities at modest cost.

Don't put too much faith in the camper's door locks either. Remove any easily portable valuables to the security of your home.

If you must park in less protected locations, avoid dark side streets and places where crooks can carry on their activities unobserved.

During trips it is smart to treat your camper as you would your home: when you're away, leave an interior light on to suggest someone is inside or nearby. Close and secure all windows and vents. Don't neglect protection for five minutes. It could cost you your camper and your vacation.

Keep a written record of your camper's contents. Also note the camper's identification-plate number, as well as dents, scratches, and other markings useful in identifying it. (A photo of your rig is an excellent idea.) Some owners paint a huge number on the rooftop, virtually invisible from ground level, but easily spotted by patroling aircraft (thieves may not even realize it's up there.)

How to Keep Your Trailer from Wandering

If you are among the millions who own trailers for camping, boating, snowmobiling, transporting horses, or general utility use, you have a twofold security problem: how to secure your trailer while it is in tow, and how to safeguard it while parked apart from your car.

Leaving an unhitched trailer on your driveway or at a campsite, etc., is a wide-open invitation to loss. Thieves need only drive up to it, couple the trailer to their car (which takes just seconds) — and drive away with it.

Much the same problem exists when a trailer coupled to your car is left unattended, an easy prey to rip-off artists armed with bolt cutters. It takes little effort to unhitch your trailer, transfer it to the thieves' car, and make a quick getaway.

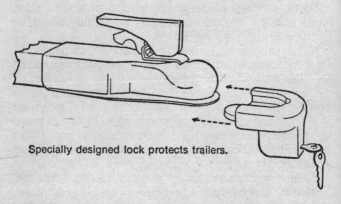

Specially designed lock protects trailers.

The best protection for unhitched trailers is the specialized lock that completely blocks access to the coupler cavity. Make sure the lock is steel, not an easily broken casting. Also see that it incorporates pin-tumbler locking the same as a high-security padlock. Master Lock's unit (shown) comes in five sizes to fit a wide variety of boat, camping, horse and utility trailers.

For on-vehicle protection, the need is maximum resistance to cutting, sawing, and prying. Since the size of the locking eye in your trailer hitch dictates the maximum shackle size you can use, look for a special lock designed with trailers in mind, such as

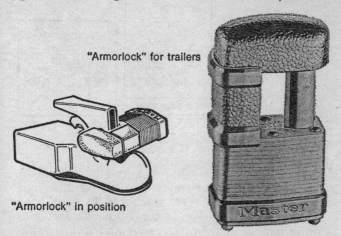

"Armorlock" for trailers

"Armorlock" in position

the "Armorlock" shown here. This will greatly increase protection against loss. Note that the Armorlock shackle is encased in ¾-inch armor — too thick to fit in the jaws of most bolt cutters. Most importantly, the double-locking design makes it all but impossible to pry the shackle from the case. Rugged laminated case construction resists smashing.

Protecting Outboard Motors

Millions of valuable outboard motors are secured to boats by clamp screws that make them almost as vulnerable to theft as an unlocked bicycle. Simply turn two handles and walk away with the motor.

While all sorts of improvised locking methods have been tried by uneasy owners, a better answer is to invest in one of the powerful outboard motor locks designed expressly to protect your motor against theft. The simple and effective lock shown here is made by Master Lock and consists of a slotted hardened-steel tube designed to slide over the

Outboard motor clamps cannot be turned with tube in position.

Slip tube over clamp handles

Lock tube securely in place

tightened clamp screw handles and lock them in place so that thieves cannot turn the handles and the motor remains firmly anchored to your boat transom. High security features to look for: pin-tumbler locking mechanism; tube and lock shackle of case-hardened steel; marine design that provides extra protection against weather and water.

Do Not Let Valuable Skis Walk Away

One sure way to encourage your skis to vanish is to follow the common practice of sticking them in a snowbank when you stop at a store or bar. Thieves are delighted. Especially favored are the short, popular skis — and the more expensive, the better.

Many hundreds of thousands of dollars worth of skiing equipment gets ripped off each season because of this kind of owner thoughtlessness. Records show that eight out of ten ski thefts involve carelessly handled, unlocked, unattended equipment. A few simple precautions can prevent this kind of needless loss:

Don't leave skis unlocked or unattended even for 30 seconds.

Use coin-operated locking ski racks, or commercial ski cable locks.

When using cable locks, take the time to install them properly and tightly.

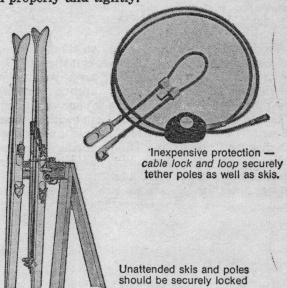

Inexpensive protection — *cable lock and loop* securely tether poles as well as skis.

Unattended skis and poles should be securely locked

Do not leave skis out overnight, even when locked in coin-operated racks. Most racks can be broken open in less than a minute by thieves under cover of darkness. The spot for them is right there in your hotel room.

If you must leave skis in a car, conceal them in the trunk if there is sufficient room. Or lock them inside the passenger compartment. Never leave them stashed outside the car on a carrier, even one that locks.

Mark your skis with your name. Better yet, have your identification engraved on them.

When you must "park your skis" — LOCK THEM SECURELY as you would a bicycle. Use a cable lock that protect both the *skis and poles* by anchoring them to a post, tree, or other strong, immovable object.

Be Ready to Act if Trouble Strikes

This recommendation seems so elementary as to be passed over in giving advice. But the truth is few of us think to keep a record of our valuables. Write down serial numbers and unique identifying features. And permanently mark your valuables (TV sets, typewriters, bikes, radios, etc.) with your social security number or driver's license number to aid tracing and identifying stolen goods. Many police departments offer the public free use of a scriber under their "Operation Identification" programs (see chapter 5).

Chapter 9

Around the House

The isolated house, unlighted, invisible from the road, with no one at home, is a burglar's dream. It gives him the privacy he needs for his work, plenty of time, and relatively little risk.

The opposite, of course, is his nightmare. A house with alert neighbors who care, one flooded with light and easily observable at all times, is the kind a thief is likely to pass by.

Surroundings for Safety

Let There Be Light

Light serves many purposes for your protection. Principally, it gives an intruder pause, since someone may be at home. While lights do not necessarily mean someone is in the house, the lack of lights at night is an almost sure giveaway that the house is empty.

The most important places to light are your front doors and yard. This allows you to see who is ringing the bell or knocking at your door, and it protects you when you return after dark. If you keep a light burning at all outside entrances, you effectively deny an intruder the darkness he wants for cover. It is remarkably inexpensive insurance. In spite of today's high cost of energy, it only costs a nickel or so to burn a 60-watt bulb for twelve hours.

Important: Do not let outside lights burn during the daylight hours. This is an unmistakable tip-off that no one is home to turn them off.

Light should cover all points where an intruder can gain entry. Outside lights should illuminate the area around your house so that a person can be visible, but they should not shine into your neighbor's house to keep him awake at night.

The front of your house should be lighted whenever you are away, if only to protect yourself when you return. The light should be sufficient to allow you to read your wristwatch.

If there is an especially enclosed area, a window or doorway among trees or bushes, or a porch, light this from inside the house. This applies especially to alleys between houses or between a house and a fence. If possible, bathe the whole house in light.

Lights should be attached to the eaves, the corner of the house, an outside structure or pole set into the ground. Outside lights located away from the building should have wires underground, preferably running through a one-inch pipe. The switches should be located inside the house, preferably at one spot. Be sure to use outside fixtures approved by Underwriters Laboratory (U.L.).

It is a good practice to wire the lights so that they go on automatically when the alarm system is triggered. This adds another dimension of danger for the thief who hopes to break in, grab, and run before the police arrive.

It is also a good idea to install a multiple switch system that permits you to turn on lights all over the house at one turn of a switch. The sudden bathing of the entire house in light, in case of a break-in or unusual emergency, is comforting to the owner and is more than even a seasoned burglar is likely to want to cope with.

There is one light you can leave on all night and which will indicate to any passing would-be intruder that someone is home: the bathroom light. That's one room that may be in use at any hour of the night!

Encourage your neighbors to keep their outside lights on at least until midnight. A brightly lighted neighborhood is a powerful deterrent to an intruder.

Neighborly Cooperation

One of the most civilized and helpful elements of community living is the reliance we can have on our neighbors — and vice versa. It is certainly a comforting feeling to know that your neighbor will keep a watchful eye on your house while you are away, in exchange for the same kind of interest on your part while his house is empty. A neighborly call to the police, or a warning call directly to the neighbor about a sinister figure lurking in the yard, can go a long way toward protecting everyone's life and property.

Landscaping, Shrubbery and Fencing

As beautiful as thick bushes and shrubbery may look around a home, it is not a good idea to have so much greenery around that a trespasser can approach your house without being seen, either from the street or from inside. A concealed approach route, and bushes to hide behind, are very appealing to the intruder who wants to get near to or into your home. Keep shrubs and bushes especially low and well-trimmed around windows and doors.

Fencing around a home presents a balancing act between security and esthetics for most people. No one wants to live in a house that looks like a prison or a factory. Hedges are a good compromise, but if they are high enough to restrain an intruder, they are high enough to hide him from passersby.

Buildings Not Connected with the House

Storage buildings and unattached garages can be very attractive targets for burglars. Some thieves even specialize in hitting such types of buildings, rather than houses, because the stealable merchandise is usually quite valuable, and the homeowner may not even be aware of a loss for days or weeks after the crime has been committed. By then, it is usually too late even to determine exactly when the loss occurred, and the thief has long since been able to get rid of the goods. Seasonal clothes, sports equipment, gardening or snow-removing machinery, and many other pieces of costly equipment may be stashed away, unthought of by the owner until each piece is actually needed.

To keep the possibility of theft at a minimum, you should light all outer buildings and equip them with top-quality locks. Doors and windows should be protected just as they are in the main house, and all hasps and padlocks must reflect the quality and security your property deserves. It is a good idea to have an internal lighting system that can be turned on or off from the house. This can be especially effective and helpful in keeping the garage free of passersby. A low-cost alarm system can also be a splendid way of making sure you're alerted to any unauthorized attempt to enter these outer buildings.

General Appearance and Common Sense

"If you've got it, flaunt it" may be an appropriate slogan in some cases, but when it comes to protecting your home, "Cool it and keep it" might be a better suggestion. Wealthy *looking* homes are apt to attract characters who feel that the potential loot is worth the risk. This is not to recommend that you purposely create an atmosphere of utter neglect. But it does stand to reason that it makes good sense to go easy on showing off. And that also means making sure that rumors of vast wealth or verbal pictures of valuable collections of antiques or coins or what-have-you are not bandied about where neighborhood gossip can pick them up. Cool it, with a nice "average" outward appearance, and you'll be less likely to be ripped off.

Some Miscellaneous Thoughts about Your Home

The number of your house should be well lighted at night. Not only does this make for easy identification for people looking for you, but it eliminates strangers coming up to the door asking you what your house number is. If you should have to call the police, it will be mighty helpful to have the house number clearly visible, too.

Extension phones are great. You should have sufficient extensions, easily available in convenient locations, so that one is always nearby in case you need to reach a phone in an emergency.

Locks on internal doors, especially bedrooms, are a good idea. If you should hear an intruder at night and can lock him *out* of your bedroom, he's apt to take off rather than to break down your bedroom door.

It is a good idea to lock your car, with the windows securely rolled up, even when it is in the garage or especially when it is in the driveway of your home. Plenty of cars have been stripped or stolen by brazen thieves while their owners have been blissfully unaware of what was going on right outside their doors.

Never leave the garage door open when you leave, even if you plan to be gone only a few minutes. To anyone considering a break-in, an empty garage is an immediate tip-off that no one is home. And the open door gives him easy access.

Chapter 10

On the Street

"Street Gang Harasses
Pedestrians and Shopkeepers"

"New York, Oct. 10: A gang of some forty young toughs ranged unchecked through parts of midtown Manhattan for nearly half an hour last night, robbing strollers of money and jewelry, breaking store windows and stealing merchandise from shops.

"Responding to telephone calls for help from anguished victims, police arrived on the scene and arrested 11 of the youths. The balance of the offenders scattered and escaped as police cars drove up. Those arrested were charged with assault, harrassment and malicious mischief. Because of their ages, none of the arrested youngsters was identified by police.

"According to eyewitness reports, the youths formed a veritable wave of terror as they swooped along the sidewalks of Seventh Avenue from 39th Street to 47th Street, starting about 11:00 o'clock. One couple reported being surrounded by a mob of yelling and screaming boys who forced the man to surrender his gold watch and his wallet, while his wife had to relinquish her purse and a ruby ring. One store-owner described the group as a bunch of 'marauding' animals."

Millions of men, women, and children in every city in the world walk the streets, stroll along the avenues, and enjoy the sights and activities that go

on around them. A few get mugged, robbed, even
kidnapped. To a large extent, the victim of a street
crime is a matter of chance. However, some things
you do or do not do will increase your chances of
becoming a victim. And a few things you can do will
lessen the loss.

On the Streets

All of us walk the streets — most of us without
fear. But there are times and places where one needs
to recognize the possibility of crime. The advice in
this chapter seems obvious, but too often we forget
these elements of caution.

The first rule for a pedestrian is to carry no more
cash than you need to. But to keep a mugger from
becoming enraged, it is a good idea to carry at least
ten dollars. Most of those who are inclined to attack
to steal from you have a great need and are easily
frustrated to a point where they lose their sense of
reason. An unsuccessful mugging often leads to a
violent attack on the victim.

The idea is (1) to reduce the temptation to a thief
and the amount of your loss, (2) to have enough
money to avoid frustrating a junkie and cause him
to assault you.

Hiding cash was grandma's way of seeking safety
and it still has advantages. There are no pockets in
underwear, but a money belt is still available and
some people manage to hide money on their persons.
If you have a substantial amount of money, such as
for a bank deposit, carry it separately from your
purse or wallet.

Before You Leave Home

If you are one of those people who feel insecure
about going around without a substantial sum of
money, carry traveler's checks for any sum you
might want.

Remember that credit cards are valuable to a crook, often more valuable than cash. Some wallets are so arranged that all the credit cards show when you open the clasp; others that show one at a time make you less conspicuous when you pay a bill.

When a credit card elapses, or when you decide you are not going to use it anymore, destroy it. It has your name behind it as long as it is whole.

Don't Be a Standout

It almost goes without saying that you are safest when you do not attract attention to yourself. If you are carrying a good deal of money to pay a bill or to buy something, keep the large bills in a separate buttoned or zippered pocket. Keep small bills for car fare, lunch, etc., in a handy place so that a large amount of cash doesn't show.

Some crime-wise people say that you can be virtually invisible when you walk the streets by not calling attention to yourself. Do not wear flashy jewelry or clothes. If you like to be "different," be different in a conservative way while you are on the streets. If you are going to a party wearing all your finery, take a cab and do not stop at an unfamiliar bar on the way.

Another caution about your clothes: when you are out walking, wear clothing that allows freedom of movement. However, avoid easy to grab loose scarves, capes, or straps. Wear shoes that you are able to run in.

Use a money clip rather than a wallet. Keep small bills in a separate pocket. Never flash a roll of bills. If you are paying for purchases, take out of your pocket or purse approximately the amount you need. To a thief, a roll of bills gets as much attention as waving a red flag at a bull!

Safe Deposits

It is a good idea to vary your check-cashing routine. Do not cash your check at the same place and at the same time.

Paydays, the first and the fifteenth of the month, and Social Security days are particularly dangerous. You can have Social Security checks sent to, and deposited in, your bank account merely by filling out a form at your local bank. It is the safest, wisest procedure. You can be paid with a check which you can mail to your bank or you can have a bank account near where you work so that excess cash can be deposited immediately and in the company of fellow workers.

Watch Your Step

Select a route with the brightest light and greatest traffic. Walk with confidence, at a steady pace. Look as if you know where you are going. If possible, be familiar with your route. Avoid dark streets or alleys. Keep away from doorways and unlighted parking lots or high shrubbery. If necessary, walk as near to the curb as possible, away from doorways, but not so close to the curb that a motorist can grab you.

If there is reason to be suspicious of the building entrances, walk in the middle of the street; but, of course, be on the lookout for oncoming cars. Remember, doorways and shrubbery can be hiding places. Parked cars and even passing cars can be a danger.

Nighttime walking requires special precautions. Obviously, one does not stroll on deserted streets or in high-crime areas. If you must go into such areas, take someone along with you.

Avoid any bar, restaurant or nightclub where you are not well known, especially in the more crime-prone parts of town.

If there is a group of suspicious people in your way, walk around them rather than through. Cross to the other side of the street well in advance of the group if possible. Try not to appear conspicuous in your avoidance action, but act naturally. Like animals, criminals detect fear.

While You Are Walking

Be especially alert if you are stopped for information. One technique is to divert your attention with a question while a confederate snatches your purse or attaché case.

Know where there is a police call box in your neighborhood and know how to use it.

If you expect to be out after dark, carry a pocket flashlight.

When you reach home, don't stop to pick up your mail at night. Approach a vestibule, keys in hand, and get the door closed behind you as quickly as you can.

Women should not go to bars or cocktail lounges at night without an escort or female companion. Otherwise, one is just asking for trouble.

In Public Transportation

Usually there are many people with you when you are using a bus, streetcar, or the subway. The bus is the safest of these. Sit close to the doors. However, on the platform or in the waiting area, late at night or even on Sundays and holidays, you may find yourself alone or virtually alone. Be alert.

In high-crime areas, consider taking a taxi, at least for the part of the way that is most deserted.

In any vehicle, do not fall asleep. Watch for the open window that might make your purse or a package vulnerable. Select the car on a subway where there is a conductor. Never allow yourself to be the only one on a subway car. Move to the next car that has people.

If possible, arrange to have someone meet you at the end of the line, especially if you must pass through an area that is likely to be unfamiliar or somewhat dangerous for a single individual.

If you ask, a cabdriver or friend who drives you home will be glad to wait until you are safely inside.

How to Avoid Pickpockets

Unlike burglars, pickpockets work during the day or night, particularly in crowds. They love crowds.

Whenever you are in a crowd, on the street, in a shop, on the subway, especially at a big gathering like a fair, you are a target for a pickpocket.

You cannot overestimate the skill with which trained pickpockets operate. There are actually schools which train pickpockets from early youth so that they can remove a set of keys from a pants pocket without setting off a set of bells sewed to the edges, remove a wristwatch while you are wearing it, or lift a wallet from an inside pocket, all without attracting your attention. One sure giveaway, however, is being bumped in a crowd.

A standard operation often involves four people. One stands in front of the victim, one pushes from behind, a third lifts the valuables and passes it to a fourth who is out of range if a complaint should be made.

Some pickpockets use a newspaper or handkerchief as a cover to hide their movements.

What can you do?

You can be especially alert if you are in a crowd. Do not carry much money in a wallet. A buttoned pocket is a safer place to keep a wallet. Keep it in the inside pocket of your jacket and keep the jacket buttoned. Otherwise keep the wallet in your pocket, angled slightly so that it must be straightened to be removed. In a congested area, keep your hand in a pocket over your wallet, or fold your arms over your chest to cover pockets inside your suit coat. If you are bumped, don't automatically reach for your wallet. The pickpocket may just be trying to find out for sure where you carry your money.

If You Come upon a Riot

In times and places where demonstrations, or even riots, are precipitated, some consideration should be given to this danger. The innocent bystander is in as much danger as the active participants.

First advice is to *stay away* or *go away*. This is for real, not a television show or movie. If you must get to the other side, go around the crowd. If you must watch events, get into a building in the area which is removed from the center of conflict. If you are a witness to a crime, phone the police. Do not step forward into the battle itself.

If You Are Being Followed

If you have to get off a bus or subway at a point where there are few people, notice if you are being followed and take the necessary precautions. For example, after you have left the bus or subway, walk about twenty steps to see if someone else is following, changing direction abruptly to see if the suspected follower does too. Look in a store window, pause, and check the reflection, if there is one.

If a person is following, you (1) look for a police officer or (2) go into a lighted store and call for one, or (3) if approached, scream. Any officer who responds will understand, but anyone who is following you will be off and running long before that. If you see a cab, hail it and get in.

In an emergency, look for a car with its door button in an unlocked position. Duck in, lock the door, and lean on the horn until help comes.

Screaming is an effective deterrent. You may feel like a nut, but what assailant wants to tangle with a nut?

If you feel you are in immediate danger, drop your wallet into a mailbox. You will be violating a law, but you will probably get it back.

Do not, if possible, go into a strange building. If you feel threatened, there is actually more safety in the street than in any enclosed place.

If you live nearby, walk, do not run home, unless you feel an attack is imminent. When you do duck into your house, you must give yourself just enough time to make a good escape. You do not want to take a thief home with you.

If Someone Stops You

Remember, that the average street thief is probably as nervous as you are. He is risking a jail term. However, in big cities, such street criminals are often very young and very reckless. Don't get suckered into a doorway, or side street, or an unlighted parking lot. A common ploy is a request by a woman who says she needs help with a sick companion. Instead of investigating yourself, call the police.

An attacker may have an emotional or mental problem which induces him to want to injure his victim. If you are attacked, swift response and action is your best defense. Scream. Scream "Fire!" It attracts attention and will bring people who hesitate to get involved with a cry for help. Do not be afraid to be considered a nut. The thief certainly does not want to get involved with one, and a little embarrassment will not hurt you. Do not fight unless you are in definite physical danger, and do not fight without a strong defense.

You must, of course, use your best judgment. If attacked in a relatively defenseless situation, give up your valuables quickly and without an argument. Never argue with a gun or knife. Try not to panic; there's plenty of time to fall apart afterward. Do not make any fast moves. If you have to reach for a wallet, tell the thief what you are doing.

Weapons for Defense

Notwithstanding your first instincts, weapons are a poor defense against street crimes. The thief has sized you up as a weaker adversary. You are taken by surprise. You will have difficulty reaching for a weapon unless you are exceptionally fast and quick-witted. You will, in all likelihood, have a weapon pointing at you.

Every purse and pocket has some weapons that can be useful if you want to use them: a ballpoint pen, a comb, a nail file, keys. An umbrella with its point or a tightly rolled newspaper can be used to poke at a face.

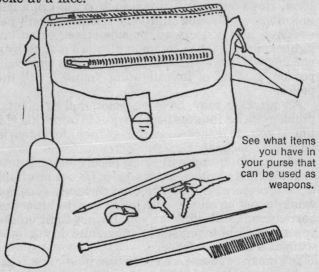

See what items you have in your purse that can be used as weapons.

An attacked person is vulnerable in several spots. But most people have to overcome being squeamish about hurting anyone. Do not hesitate to bite or poke at an eye, ear, or nose.

Fight dirty. Kick, stick a finger in an eye, strike for the Adam's apple, go for the genital area with a purse or your knee, stomp on a foot, punch directly into the ear. All these blows can have a devastating effect on an assailant.

A knee jab to the groin can be totally disabling to a male attacker. The knee must come up hard and unexpectedly between the legs.

An elbow jab to the groin is more difficult to give but can be just as effective. Drop to a sideways crouch and clasp your hands together. As your attacker approaches, rise and swing hard, using your back and leg muscles.

Long fingernails directed to the eyes can be very deadly. Pressure on the eye sockets will loosen an assailant's grip.

Some defenses will not win the battle for you but may distract an attacker long enough to let you get away. These include:

> Pulling hair, on the head or beard.
> Grabbing hard at a necklace or anything around the neck — tie, beads, or chain or earrings.
> A hard spit in the face, especially to the eyes.
> A kick in the shin, especially with a heavy or sharp shoe.
> Whenever and wherever you can: bite!

Bear in mind that the attacker has already decided that you are vulnerable to his intentions. He may likely have a weapon or a better weapon than you have. Run if at all possible. Scream if anyone will hear you or just scream anyway to scare the attacker enough to make a run for it. Screaming directly into someone's face is enough to make him stand still long enough to give you a chance to run like crazy. If pursued, turn on the attacker with a short burst of blows and kicks. Then run some more.

Nevertheless, there are some safeguards.

A "police" whistle worn on the wrist of the hand not engaged with your purse is sometimes effective. Do not wear it around your neck, because it could become a noose or at least the source of a deep cut if it is seized by an attacker.

Learning certain self-defense techniques such as karate or judo does not guarantee that you will never be harassed. However, knowledge and practice of these techniques will help to reduce your chances of being hurt. The objective, first, is not to beat your opponent, but to surprise him by resisting in an intelligent, swift fashion. Then give him the opportunity to flee from *you*.

When You Cannot Fight

Often it is obvious that the odds make fighting senseless. If it is property that the thief is after, give it up willingly; he will get it anyway.

Sometimes an attacker is much more interested in roughing you up. The best defensive position for the defenseless is on the ground, knees drawn up to protect your stomach, hands clasped covering your head. You will probably be hurt, but less so than if you tried to fight three or four hoodlums.

Quite simply, there is no guarantee you will not be hurt whether you choose to fight off an attacker or surrender. You must make the judgment for yourself. But if you *think* of yourself as defenseless, you *are* defenseless. In reality, you never are.

Good judgment, a clear head, and holding to the conviction that you have the ability to defend yourself is the key to your survival.

Chapter 11

When You Are Away

"No April Foolin"

"Mrs. George Wilson will remember this year's April Fool's Day for a long time. The 76-year-old widow watched yesterday as a young man carried a TV set across her neighbor's path to a waiting truck. She rushed out to ask if the set was being taken in for repairs. When he replied, "Yes," Mrs. Wilson asked him to please take hers, too. He was happy to oblige her.

"A few hours later, Mrs. Wilson saw a police car in her neighbor's driveway. Eager to find out what happened, she learned her neighbor's house had been burglarized. Among the items stolen was a brand new color TV set."

Funny, sure! But it could happen to you.

Publicity

If you are leaving home for a few days, tell your neighbors, so they can keep an eye on your house. You will do the same for them while they are away. But do not make a public announcement about your being away. Mentioning it at the cleaners, or to the rubbish removal man, to a delivery boy, or in the supermarket may invite a most unwelcome visitor. Publicity through society announcements or local news stories can be just as bad. The chances of your being burglarized are increased by such publicity.

It is a good idea to avoid publicizing anything about your home that might be of interest to a prospective thief. Stories about coin collections, stamps, or other valuables should not be broadcast by any members of your family.

But even without specific attractions, your home is more vulnerable when you are away than when you are in it. And spreading the word that you are off for a weekend or for a vacation increases your chances of being hit by thieves.

Making Your Home More Secure While You Are Away

The first rule is not to let newspapers, mail, and other items accumulate on your front porch. To minimize the number of strangers who know about your absence, ask a neighbor to pick up your mail daily and to check for advertising flyers that appear on your front door.

Uncollected items on the doorstep
are a sure sign that no one is home.

Especially in a large city, do not call the newspaper's circulation department to tell them you will be away. Either tell the paper boy, who will adjust his daily order without revealing your address, or call the paper and cancel your subscription. It is easy to start it up again when you return. And be sure to arrange for lawn care in the summer and snow removal in the winter to help make the house look occupied.

Do not discontinue your phone service. The disconnect message which is automatically given when anyone dials your number is a dead giveaway that you are gone. It is a good idea to turn down the volume of your telephone bell; so it will not be a clue that no one is home.

If you are gone just for the evening, leave a light on in one or two rooms, according to your normal living pattern. Turn a radio on, loud enough to be heard at the front or back door.

"This House Is Protected"

Decals can help deter a thief. If your house is equipped with an alarm of any kind, put stickers in prominent places (outside windows and doors) announcing that the house is protected. If your equipment and belongings are marked with police identification numbers, be sure the stickers say so. And if there is a dog on the premises, a big "BEWARE OF DOG" sign may be useful.

Since there is no sure way to keep everyone from knowing you are away, some people resolve the problem by inviting a professional "house-sitter" to live in their homes while they are away for lengthy periods of time. The natural caution to observe with house-sitters is to make sure they themselves are trustworthy and reliable. Checking references and making specific arrangements are absolutely vital.

Get together with your neighbors and agree to keep an eye on each other's homes. If anyone sees anything suspicious, the police should be called. Every reasonable effort should be made to get a good description and the license number of any intruder in the neighborhood. Sometimes a burglar will brazenly back a truck up to a residence and carry off valuable possessions. If your neighbors have not said anything about moving, be suspicious. Call the police.

Store valuables — especially coin or stamp collections, or jewelry — in a safe-deposit box while you're gone.

When using an automatic timer to turn on lights, remember in the fall and winter it gets dark inside very early. Be sure light is scheduled to turn on when anyone at home would need it.

Do NOT leave an outside light on all day. And do NOT leave shutters closed and drapes drawn. Both are sure signs that no one is home.

If you have an alarm system, make sure that one or more neighbors (and possibly the police, too) know how it works and what to do if it sounds.

Ask a neighbor or a close friend to come by and check your house from time to time. This includes being sure that the furnace is working properly, no lights are mistakenly left on, there's no water dripping, etc.

It is a good idea to move valuable possessions like paintings or silver if they can be seen from the outside. The combination of an empty house and a valuable temptation may be too much for a casual viewer to resist.

Above all, do NOT leave a note on your front door or in your mailbox saying when you will be back, even from a brief afternoon outing.

Lights Inside Are Helpful

Most security experts agree that some interior lights should be kept on in the house most of the time. The cost is small and a cursory passing look will indicate that someone may be at home. Even when you go to sleep, it is a good practice to have a light on somewhere in the house, visible from the outside. If you select a different room every night you may discourage an intruder, as most are reluctant to go into a house where someone may be awake.

More About Timers

Timer lights that go on and off at normal hours, in line with your regular living schedule, should be set up whenever you are going to be away from home for a few days or more. Arrange at least two different sets — one in the living area and one in the bedroom part of the house — to operate at different hours.

An inexpensive timer is excellent home protection.

Electric timers work by a clock that you can set at predetermined hours. Your timer can be used to turn your radio on and off, as well as your lights. Do not attach a timer to a television set, however, as there may be danger of fire. The same holds for air conditioners.

When You Travel

As soon as you leave home, you leave certain types of security behind you. It is difficult to get assistance if you have an accident or become ill.

Traveler's checks are a big help. They are safer than cash. If you lose them, they will be replaced. Almost any business house or bank will exchange them into cash for you.

Don't overpack. Luggage that is overpacked can be opened just by being dropped "accidentally." Avoid carrying expensive luggage. Their locks are not much better than those on less costly suitcases, and a thief may be tempted because he reasons that an expensive suitcase will yield better loot.

If you are traveling with a camera or a camera bag, remember the section on purse snatching. Check your camera whenever it is a nuisance to carry. Do not put your camera equipment in your baggage. Carry it with you. If you do not want to do that, ask the hotel clerk to put it in the vault until you want to reclaim it. Do not leave it in your hotel room.

About Cash

Cash is important in every phase of your life. For some people, carrying a lot of cash is a confidence builder or something that will impress people. But remember the earlier warning about flashing a roll of bills. It attracts thieves. In such cases, it is a hazard to life and limb.

If you are a big spender and even if you are not, a credit card is a useful thing to have. The recognized ones are so universally accepted that you do not have to carry substantial amounts of cash these days anywhere in the world. After you have paid a bill, make sure your credit card is returned to you, and that it is yours, not someone else's.

A checking account will help to take care of many purchases, but personal checks are often not acceptable without considerable identification. Sometimes, even then, they are refused.

When you pay a bill or check into a hotel, be careful not to unroll a wad of cash or a long string of credit cards. Credit card thefts have increased considerably of late, for those small pieces of plastic are more valuable to thieves than large amounts of cash.

Hotel-Room Security

Rooms in most modern hotels, both in the United States and abroad, are secured at night by a bolt lock as well as the regular snap lock. A rubber wedge under the door or a chair placed under the knob will provide an additional safeguard. However, while you are away, your room is definitely vulnerable.

As we have stressed, you should not keep valuables in your room. All hotels provide vaults for cash or jewelry. It is best to take advantage of that free service to protect your portable valuables. If you insist on leaving your camera or a radio in your hotel room, at least lock it in your suitcase. True, the whole suitcase can be stolen, but a piece of luggage can be conspicuous and the impulse-appeal to a sneak thief is reduced when a camera is out of sight.

Some people put a "Do Not Disturb" sign on their door and trust to luck. It is not much protection.

One effective and useful lock favored by hotel guests is made by Yale, called a "Travelok". This clever device can be attached to doors and drawers to provide extra security. It can be applied to doors that open either inward or outward, and locked from

Take your own security with you when you are away from home. Yale Disc Tumbler Travel Lock. Courtesy Eaton Corporation.

the outside. On a chest of drawers, the Travelok will securely fasten the top drawer and thus protect small items that you might leave in it.

During the day, when you are away from your room, hotel security is limited, to say the least. Many people in the hotel have passkeys — cleaning people, housekeepers, other personnel — and practically anyone requesting a key from the front desk is likely to get it. With your room so utterly vulnerable, it just does not make sense to leave anything of value behind while no one is there. While the odds are against your being ripped off, the possibility is so great that it is simply not worth taking any unnecessary chances.

The Trunk of Your Car

The trunk of your car, but not the passenger compartment, is a relatively safe place to keep luggage and clothing on a trip. But if your car is not in a garage at night, it is a good idea to take your luggage into your room with you. It is very simple for a thief to jimmy open the trunk of a car parked outside motel rooms. With a strong crowbar, it might take him five seconds or so.

Carelessness Can Be Expensive

Part of the fun of a leisurely vacation drive is to stop at various places on the way — to eat, to shop, to explore, or to admire the landscape. How often have you seen an entire family pile out of the car, leaving windows open and doors unlocked, and cameras, portable radios, binoculars, and other valuables scattered in great profusion. When they return to the car after only a few minutes, all too often the story is the same: someone has simply reached in and helped himself to whatever was sitting there unwatched and unprotected.

The moral: Do NOT leave a vacation car unlocked, even "for just a minute." It doesn't take a sneak thief even that long to do his dirty work.

Children Need Special Attention

When you travel with children, they should wear identification to indicate their name, the local place of residence, and the phone number. Update the tag for each city where you stop. For young children, and even for adults, the trauma of being lost can play terrible tricks on one's memory.

Common Sense at the Airport

It is up to you to claim your baggage, and to make sure you get your own. In some airports, guards compare the stub of your baggage claim ticket and the suitcase you have selected. Even if you claim the baggage later, you have to prove your identity and your right to the piece of luggage you ask for. But in some other airports, the security system is very lax. Even when there is careful screening of baggage taken directly from the carousel, unclaimed baggage is frequently treated with some degree of casualness. If you delay claiming your luggage, to meet with friends or to have a drink, you may find that someone else has helped himself to your bags.

When you land, claim your baggage immediately. Make sure that any damage claim or insurance claim (especially for bags which may have been insured for excess value) is registered right away. Remember: an airline's liability for most luggage is limited to five hundred dollars. Know what is in your bag and decide if you need additional coverage before you check your baggage through.

Be Reachable

While you are away, you should still be able to be reached. Leave an itinerary with a relative, friend, or neighbor. If possible, also leave a key to your house with the local police or a neighbor, or both. If you have an alarm system, leave instructions on how to turn it off.

Before you leave, let the police know that you will be away and tell them the name of the person who knows how to reach you and of whoever has the keys.

If you're off to a remote spot for hunting or camping, you are particularly vulnerable. Let someone at home know exactly where you will be so the state police or rangers will be able to find you. You may even arrange to call at a specified time. Let someone like a ranger or local police know you are going to be in a particular remote area with which they are familiar. You never know when you may need help.

Chapter 12

Your Car
and You

*"Car thefts are increasing, mostly because
the costs of new cars and spare parts have
risen so markedly that the illegal trafficking
in stolen cars and parts has become extra-
ordinarily lucrative.*

"The statistics are staggering.

*"A million cars are stolen in the United
States each year, ten percent of them, valued
at $163 million, in New York City. Every
day, 200 to 300 cars are stolen in the city.
Fewer than half of these are recovered."*

"If a professional thief wants your car, there's
nothing you can do to stop him. You can discourage
him, but you can't stop him," says Lt. John J. Hill,
Commander of the Police Auto Theft Squad of New
York City.

Why your car? A theft ring may have an "order"
for one like it or a ready market for the parts. Even
older cars are worth more these days, as the market
value of cars is up.

The Vulnerable Car

A car is as vulnerable to a thief as anything left
unattended on a street and, to a somewhat lesser extent, if it is in a parking lot or a garage. A
professional thief can open a car in three minutes or
less. An amateur might need ten minutes. One solu-

tion that will slow any thief down somewhat is to replace the standard door-lock buttons with the slim, tapered kind. They are almost impossible to pull up with a coat hanger.

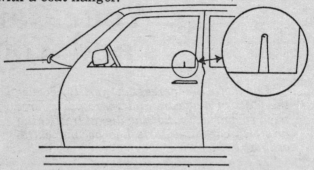

A tapered auto door lock will frustrate many car thieves.

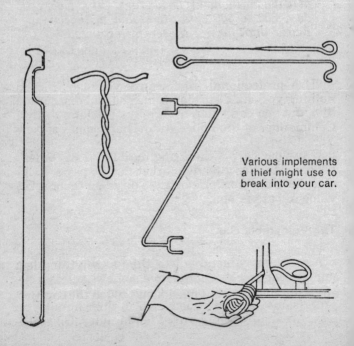

Various implements a thief might use to break into your car.

What you leave visible in the car when it is un-attended is often the final temptation. A CB radio, a tape recorder, an interestingly wrapped package, your overcoat — all are probably marketable. A jack and tire bar is all that a thief needs to steal your tires.

A thief can start your car without a key with a jumper wire under the hood or with a jiggler-type key or any of several other devices. However, over 40 percent of all cars stolen had the key in the ignition!

If you see someone tampering with your car, call the police. If the thief is about to take off, yell. Don't try to stop him on the spot.

Precautions You Can Take

First, park in a lighted, well-traveled area whenever you can. Consider whether it will be dark when you return to your car. But wherever you park, leave your car locked. At all times. Even when you are parked in your own driveway or in your garage, the doors should be locked. Over 80 percent of all cars stolen were unlocked at the time of the theft!

Get in the habit of locking your car, even if you will be away for only a few minutes.

Never leave the engine running, even for a brief moment. Many amateur thieves hang out at con-venience stores, just waiting for an unattended car with an engine running.

Your car hood should be controlled from the inside of the car, to prevent having the battery stolen. If your car is not constructed this way, consider ways of locking the hood with a chain and sturdy padlock.

When you return to your parked car, go around it to check the front and back seats and the floors, to make sure that no one is hiding in the car, before you get in. Check to see if the doors are still locked. If anything has been changed, don't touch the car. Get police help immediately.

Protect yourself by keeping an extra ignition key

(and door key) in your change purse or wallet. Keep extra ones at home, too.

Keep your gas tank filled above the quarter mark at all times. Use a locking gas-tank cap to prevent petty gas theft by siphoning.

If you are in a car and find it advisable not to get out owing to a dangerous situation that makes you nervous, honk your horn until someone calls the police. Honking in an on-and-off pattern is more effective than a steady, ear-bending, relentless blasting of the horn.

In a Garage or Parking Lot

If you must leave a key with the car, be sure you leave only the ignition key. Remove it from your key ring so you can take the other keys with you. There are two-part key rings available which makes this very simple.

Note your car's odometer mileage on the claim check, in full view of the attendant. When you return for the car, check to see that no one has gone joyriding in your car. Always take the claim check with you. Presumably your car cannot be removed from the lot without it.

Do not leave anything of value in the car. Put packages in the trunk and lock it. There are thieves who specialize in stealing from the rich collection of potential loot in cars parked in public lots. It is easy enough for one of them to look into hundreds of such cars and take his choice from whatever is available.

Long-term parking lots, such as those at airports, offer particularly attractive opportunities for car thieves. A claim check is offered automatically at the entrance gate. That ticket enables *anyone* to take a car out. If you leave the claim check in your car, especially in full view of the dash board or stuck on the sun visor, it is a simple matter for a professional to open your car and use his knowledge to get the engine started (unless you have been thoughtful enough to leave the keys under the seat or in the glove compartment) and out he can drive, paying the modest parking fee at the exit gate. Lesson: take your claim check with you.

Alone in a Car

Choose a well-lighted route with traffic, even if it is slightly longer.

Travel with windows almost entirely up and doors locked. At intersections or stoplights, allow yourself some leeway to maneuver behind the car in front of you. If accosted, lean on the horn or, if you must, go through the light, turning right. Try to keep moving.

If you cannot move, blow your horn. Use the S-O-S signal — three short, three long, three short — blasts on your horn.

If your car is stuck, put a white handkerchief on the antenna, raise the hood, and get back into the car. Lock it and wait for help. Be suspicious of anyone who offers help until you judge they are sincere and safe.

If you are alone in a car in a remote area, especially if you are a woman, and you have an accident, do not get out of the car. Let another driver come to you.

A distress signal can be an important device for anyone who drives at night. One type is a revolving beacon, powered from your cigarette lighter.

If you think you are being followed, especially if you are carrying valuables, stop at the nearest service station, call to have someone join you or ask for a police escort.

At a traffic light, keep your car in gear.

Check continuously in your rearview mirror if you have any reason to believe you are being followed. In a town or city, go around a block to verify this. If the pursuing car continues to follow you, try to catch the attention of a patrol car or drive to the nearest police station.

If threatened by a car following you, or by someone who tries to force you over, blow the horn in quick blasts. This draws more attention than just leaning on the horn. Do not be afraid to pull into a gas station or police station, blowing your horn like crazy. It may be embarrassing, but you will be safe.

A mobile telephone gives you the same protection in a car that a telephone at home does. CB radios, of course, are also very helpful, and they are considerably less expensive than a mobile telephone.

If you are parked in a strange neighborhood after dark and your car will not start, consider whether it may have been deliberately tampered with. If it appears safe to get out of the car, summon help, even if you think you can make repairs yourself. Do not accept assistance from a stranger, except perhaps to have him call someone you know for assistance. Do not allow a stranger to call a service station for you. It could be a setup.

When you are in a parked car, you are particularly vulnerable, especially in a remote area. Always park so that you can leave without difficult maneuvering. Keep doors locked and windows rolled up. In a drive-in movie, open the window only sufficiently to receive and hold the speaker.

If Your Car Suddenly Just Will Not Go

Pull the car off to the side of the road if you possibly can. Get as far to the right as you are able, and try not to block any traffic lanes. If it is safe, passengers should get out of the car and stay off the road. Stay with the car until help comes. For safety's sake, and to attract the attention of a patrol car, do the following:

Tie a white handkerchief to radio antenna or front left window.

Turn blinker lights on to warn traffic.

Raise the hood.

Set out one or two flares, about fifty feet behind your car.

If you have a mobile telephone or CB radio, call for help.

If you are off the road and are qualified to do so, try to make repairs.

If the car is stalled, and you cannot hear the starter motor when you turn it on, possibly because of a defective battery, turn off the radio, heater or air conditioner, and, if safe, the lights, and try again. Tapping the battery cables with a heavy instrument sometimes helps.

If you are alone and a stranger offers to help, be on guard. It is better to ask that the highway patrol be notified.

Car Antitheft Steps to Take

It is easy to install a car alarm. A hidden alarm switch sounds the alarm if anyone tampers with the doors, windows, trunk, a hubcap, or antenna.

Electronic alarms connect with the car's horn and can flash headlights or cut off the ignition if doors and windows are opened prior to your turning a special key.

Do not use a warning sticker with a car alarm system. The sticker alerts a potential car thief and suggests that he should disconnect the alarm system before he goes to work on your car. Any car thief worth his salt will be able to discover the alarm's wires, disengage them, and then start your car without fear of setting off the alarm.

If there is no warning sticker, the thief will set off the alarm when he tries to steal your car. Although he could discover the means to disconnect the alarm, the chances are that he will take off once the alarm starts shrieking and drawing attention to what is going on.

There are other mechanisms that will help protect your car. Steering-column locks prevent the wheel gears from engaging without the key in the lock. Most new cars have these locking mechanisms.

Buzzers can be installed to warn if a key is left in the car. Shields on ignition wires make tampering more difficult. There are also special locks for car hoods, hubcaps, brake pedals, and gas tanks, or for protection against wheels being removed.

Antitheft Devices and Measures

While you cannot totally thwart a professional car thief, here are a few steps you can take to frustrate most amateurs and perhaps delay a pro:

A special fuel switch can be installed which will shut off the fuel supply if the car is stolen.

A kill switch will prevent the car from even being started unless it has been turned on by a special key.

An armored collar can be locked around the steering wheel and brake pedal by locking them together.

Removing distributor rotor is probably as simple and yet as effective a way to prevent theft as any of the more sophisticated devices. Few car thieves are likely to carry a spare rotor that will fit your car precisely. You can lock the rotor in the trunk, or take it with you. Just remember to replace it yourself before you try to start your car when you return.

Removing distributor lead. Be sure to turn the engine off before you attempt this. *Gently* lift each end of the high-tension lead that goes from the distributor to the coil and take it with you.

Antitheft devices that need installation should preferably be installed by your garage. You want to have the best installation to give you the greatest protection against knowledgeable car thieves. Unless you are an expert yourself, the cost of getting professional installation is a good and reasonable investment.

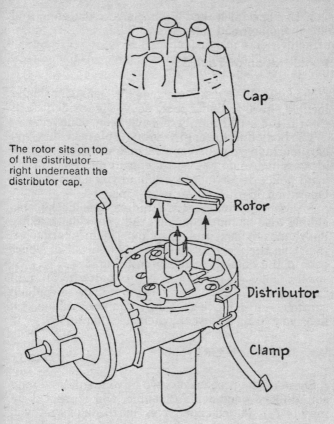

Cap

The rotor sits on top of the distributor right underneath the distributor cap.

Rotor

Distributor

Clamp

Stripping

Car thieves often do not take the whole automobile. Sometimes a gang or even an individual will scientifically strip a car of valuable parts. In the process, they leave you with a car that can be reduced to a useless hulk in a matter of minutes.

1. Park so that your car's hood faces the street or is clearly visible. Anyone tampering with your car's engine will be easily seen.
2. Park in well-lighted areas only.

3. Use special locks for wheels, and gas caps, and inside hood release.

Identification of Your Car

You should mark your car, in some specially located, hard-to-find spots, so you can identify it even if the serial numbers have been removed.

The body and the engine provide places where you can engrave your driver's license number or other identifying mark with an engraving tool. Many local police departments will lend you a tool in their Operation Identification programs.

Accessories, hubcaps, CB radios, tape decks, etc., should also be marked. You might consider making both an obvious and a hidden identification on them; so the piece can still be recognized as yours even if the obvious mark is obliterated.

Any unique marking — a pattern of nail markings, a dab of fingernail polish, a hidden scratch — in a place that only you know about can help you claim your car when it is found.

Why It Is Worth the Trouble

Some of the precautions we have mentioned may sound like a good deal of trouble, and some of them may be considered expensive. But think of what you would have to go through if your car is stolen. If you have not given it much thought, or if you believe that your insurance will immediately come across with a replacement car or a check, talk with your insurance agent. You are likely to be surprised and dismayed to learn how long it takes to settle claims these days. It is often one to three months before the company has exhausted its recovery efforts. The inconvenience can be disastrous. It makes good sense to take every possible precaution to prevent the theft in the first place.

If You See an Accident

Advise those affected that you will tell the police or the nearest service station. Unless you are certain there is no danger to yourself and that you can be helpful, simply attempt to bring in police and other emergency groups to help.

Do not move anyone who is hurt.

If someone requires first aid and no one else can provide it, by all means help. It is wise to carry a blanket and a first-aid kit in your car at all times.

Hitchhikers: NO!

Do not give lifts to strangers.

In a remote area, do not stop to help someone. Roll down your window slightly, get whatever information you need, and go for help. If someone, not a uniformed officer in a police car, asks you to pull over in a not well-frequented area, do not respond to the request even if it means colliding. Sound your horn, and drive to a service station.

If someone tries to get into your car while you are stopped, at a stoplight or for another reason, keep going, even if you have to run the light. You should have had your doors locked! If possible, turn right, sounding the horn to avoid an accident and to attract attention. Drive to a service station and report the incident and any accident.

When You Buy a Car

Thousands of stolen cars are disposed of by thieves annually. Often they are bought by careless purchasers. People who are in the market for a good used car are easy victims for professional auto thieves. Prospective buyers, quick to realize a bargain, may in their haste overlook a few general precautions. Be especially careful when buying a vehicle from a private owner. It is wisest to buy from a reputable dealer or an individual you can check out.

Be suspicious of a private seller who offers to re-register the vehicle for you, although this service might well be expected when performed by a legitimate new or used-car dealer.

Do not accept a registration as complete proof of ownership. Ask for more proof, such as the history of the auto, a bill of sale, or a previous registration certificate. Be particularly careful when an auto registered out of state is offered for sale. Never buy a car from anyone except the person listed on the registration. Do not accept a lower-priced bill of sale for tax reasons or for any other reason.

Never pay cash. Pay by personal check, money order, or bank check. This provides an automatic receipt.

The seller's name and address should be verified. Check for additional proof of identity, such as a Social Security card or driver's license.

Require a dated, witnessed bill of sale that includes the car's true price, vehicle description, including vehicle identification number, and names and addresses of both the buyer and seller. In many states you must have this information to verify the sales tax due, before license plates will be issued.

Have the car registered before you pay the seller. The State Motor Vehicle Bureau computer may reveal it to be stolen. Before purchase, ask your bank or insurance company to check the vehicle identification number for any liens against the auto and for its true ownership.

Make sure by personal inspection that the vehicle identification number on the vehicle is the same as the one listed on the bill of sale and registration certificate. Make sure it has not been altered. If it has been, report it to the police.

Chapter 13

Not for Women Only

"Teacher Is Raped Aboard IRT Train"

"An attractive French teacher, sitting alone in a subway car heading from her Brooklyn job to a Manhattan church meeting, was raped, robbed and beaten at knife-point by two young men last night.

"Her 20-minute ordeal started at 7 p.m., shortly after she boarded the deserted last car of an IRT Lexington Avenue train at the Flatbush Avenue station, near Brooklyn College where she teaches.

"A stop later, the woman found she was no longer alone. Two young men had entered the car and approached her. A knife was put to her throat and a nine-stop ride to terror started."

Reprinted by permission of the New York Post
©1977 New York Post Corporation

We call this chapter "Not for Women Only" because much of the advice is good for men as well, and, perhaps male readers will find tips of value to pass along to wives, daughters, or elderly parents.

The Woman Alone

A woman who lives alone must take some special precautions.

She should have a phone close to her bed. If possible, she should have a quick way of calling for help if it is needed.

She should have a good lock which requires an individual key on her door. A chain, preferably one with a lock, also helps.

She should have an alarm system with panic buttons at exit doors and bedside.

Most important, whenever she goes out alone, she must be alert and observant.

Finally, a loud scream is probably a woman's best deterrent to trouble.

Your Listing

An unlisted telephone number will help eliminate crank calls. But if you have a private number, don't reveal it to everybody. You will defeat its purpose.

It is safer to list your name with initials such as J. Jones, instead of Joan Jones. The same applies to your mailbox. Have your name listed with initials, not your first name.

Do not have your phone number printed on your personal stationery. This gets around, particularly in business offices, where many people see it.

Elevators

If you live in an apartment where you know the other residents and find yourself in the lobby with a stranger, let him take the elevator and wait for it to return to you. If you are on the elevator and someone gets on whose presence makes you uneasy, get off at the next floor. Stand close to the control panel and hit the alarm button if attacked. Hit any other button, too, in order to get the doors opened swiftly at any floor.

If you are waiting to go up in an elevator, don't get into one that is going down to the basement. Wait for it and catch it on the way up.

Your Telephone

Be suspicious of people who call for a date. If they tell you, "Your cousin Bill suggested I call you," check with cousin Bill.

Check the company that offers you a job if you have never heard of it before. Your library has directories that will give you a good deal of information.

Everyone gets some telephone calls that are "wrong numbers" and many people will hang up abruptly if they realize they have dialed in error. However, if you get such calls periodically, be particularly alert. Someone may be waiting for a no-answer to make sure you are not at home to interrupt a burglary. If you should receive two or three wrong numbers in a few days or over the course of a given week, tell the telephone company that you want your number changed. Let the police know it is happening, too. It is possible that you may just have a number similar to a big company or local institution.

If a caller asks for information, do not give him anything useful. Do not say, for example, that you live alone or that the man-of-the-house is away.

If the phone rings with someone who says he has a wrong number, do not give him your number. Simply ask what number he is calling and reply, "I'm sorry; that is not this number."

Sometimes a pencil or a ring tapped on the mouthpiece may suggest to the caller that the conversation is being taped. It will make a dangerous caller cautious — at the very least.

Report all nuisance or obscene calls to the telephone company. Any regular pattern deserves their attention. They have means to trace such calls, with your permission, and they will institute legal action once the party is identified.

Be particularly wary of people asking for information for a survey or regarding anything personal. If 'you feel it is legitimate, ask for their number and say you will call back. Then you can check for the name of the organization or the individual in the phone book or with information. This is particularly true if the caller claims authority from a government agency or a large well-known organization. It is wise to check.

Obscene or Nuisance Calls

Most nuisance calls are made by children and teen-agers. Hang up as soon as you are aware of the nature of the call. If the calls continue, contact the police and local telephone company representatives. Such calls are against the law. Sometimes the caller is someone in your place of work trying to get even for some unknown insult or injury.

One deterrent beyond getting the calls traced is to keep a whistle near your phone. Blow the whistle into the mouthpiece. It has a devastating effect on the caller's ear.

Verifying Nuisance or Obscene Calls

You may want to keep a record of such calls to compare with the telephone company. The following form contains some of the information it may be helpful to have.

Your Name   **Telephone Number**

Date Time How long did call last?			

Type of Call
  Obscene
  Harassing
  Threatening
  Other			

Who Was at Home at Time?
  Husband
  Wife
  Children
  Other			

Not at Home at Time
  Husband
  Children
  Wife
  Other			

Description of Caller
  Man
  Woman
  Boy (how old)
  Girl (how old)
  Silence			

Caller's Voice
  High
  Low
  Strained
  Camouflaged, Accent
  Other			

1. What in essence does the caller say?
2. Does it change when different persons answer the call?
3. Has your family had any publicity lately?
4. Is there any background noise when you receive calls?
5. Is there anyone who might want to annoy you?
6. Have you reported these calls to the police?

Purse Snatchers

Purse snatchings comprise by far the greatest number of street crimes involving stealing. The criminal requires no special skills and seldom any great courage. It is the favorite of young hoodlums who depend on their juvenile status to give them a light sentence, or none at all, if they are caught. Typically, a purse snatcher pushes you to the side, pulls hard enough to break the bag's strap, and runs.

Always hold your purse closed, under your arm, with the strap over your shoulder on the building side as you walk. If the strap is on the other side, then carry your purse with the strap across your body. Without a strap, carry the purse under your arm, holding it in your hand. (Imagine it is a football and you are going for a touchdown.)

Make a mental note of what is in your purse each day. If it is stolen, you will need to be able to identify it and its contents.

To reduce your loss from a possible purse snatching, carry extra money in a pocket or otherwise tucked away in your clothing, rather than in your purse. Credit cards, too, should be carried separately so that they are not stolen if your purse is suddenly snatched from you.

"Pockets for Women"

"SAN FRANCISCO (AP) — A 'stitching brigade' that teaches elderly women to sew secret pockets in their garments to foil would-be purse snatchers is being organized by the FBI and police.

"Law enforcement officials, in conjunction with a sewing machine company and a clothing manufacturer, are holding special classes to instruct women in the best way to frustrate handbag grabbers — simply by not carrying handbags.

"The sewing machine company provided the machines and instructor to show the women how to make hidden pockets in coat linings, and inside waistbands of pants and skirts. The clothing firm chipped in the materials."

— Miami Herald

The easiest place to keep your purse is unfortunately usually not the safest. In a restaurant, keep it on your lap. In a department store, do not put it on the counter. You must be on guard against the "grab and run" tactic. In the market, do not put your purse in the shopping cart. Carry it with you at all times.

If your purse with house keys has been snatched, you should change the door locks immediately.

When You Go Shopping

As for all your informal exposures to the world, a

basic rule for safety is to carry only as many valuables as you need.

You will need cash for many things. Charge accounts and credit cards are helpful, but they also need protecting. You do not need a lot of jewelry or the dressy mink coat that will point you out to a thief on the lookout. The more money you carry, the less extravagantly dressed you should be.

Incidentally, make sure you get your charge plates back from the clerk after any purchase.

As noted, laying a purse down on a store counter is an invitation to a snatching or a pilfering. Be especially careful in the ladies' room and in dressing rooms, where many women have had their purses ripped off.

Don't overload yourself with packages. Keep your hands and arms free, but close to your body so that nobody can easily grab you and throw you off balance. Carrying boxes and packages has three disadvantages. It marks you for attention. It offers a reward to the thief. It makes you less mobile. It is hard to run or dodge with your arms full, and it is difficult to see if your shopping bag is being pilfered. Try to get help when taking packages to your car or ask to have them delivered.

If you have a car, place your packages in the trunk and lock it. Do your shopping for valuable items last on your route.

When you return to your car after shopping, always check the back seat and glance at the floor. Sometimes attackers wait in a car for a potential victim to return.

Rape

This is the one crime women must be on the alert to avoid. Ironically, the average rapist is married, has two children, and in anywhere from 20 percent to 50 percent of all cases, is acquainted with the victim.

If statistics can be a guide, rapes occur most frequently on Sundays, in July, between 1 and 7 *a.m.* (49 percent). The frequency lessens in June, August, December, September, October, May, April, November, February, March and January, in that descending order.

The most vulnerable age groups of women are aged 16 to 20, followed by 21 to 30, 11 to 15, 31 to 40, 6 to 10, 1 to 5, 61 to 70, 51 to 60, and even 71 to 80. More than half the victims are students, and others include unemployed women, waitresses, and even prostitutes.

The victim's home is the most common scene and the assailant's home is rated next. Open spaces account for less than a quarter and automobiles rate about one in five cases.

Many rapes are never reported; so accurate statistics are virtually impossible to obtain. However, some indication of the hazards can be seen from existing statistics. A surprising element is that between 15 percent and 43 percent of all rapes involve more than one assailant, i.e., they are gang rapes.

How Do You Minimize the Chances of Being Raped?

To say a teen-ager or any young woman should never be allowed alone with a man is ridiculous. However, every woman should understand that there are real risks and that the greatest safety lies in groups of nice people.

A girl or woman increases her chances of being raped by the company she keeps, and by not being on guard against a situation that leaves her unable to escape.

When a woman is alone at home, she should not admit a stranger to the house. Never reveal that you are home alone. Keep your draperies drawn at night. Many rapists peek through windows to select a victim. Don't give him that inadvertent invitation.

When a woman is on a date, she should know something about the man and his background and, if possible, someone else should know the man and know of the specific time of the date and the planned activities, such as dinner and a film.

Who Is a Rapist?

A rapist can be your friendly next-door neighbor. A taxi driver. A complete stranger. The profile noted above indicates that most rapists know their victims and vice versa.

Rape itself is an angry, hate-filled act, rather than pure lust or passion. The rapist has a strong desire to humiliate the victim.

If Attacked

Previous chapters have discussed how to behave and what the alternatives are if attacked. One should keep a mental list of these alternatives and decide when to fight and when to run, when to scream, and when to surrender.

One defense offered is to keep talking to the rapist. Many women escape rape by talking their way out. Tell the attacker you are pregnant, or have V.D. or cancer, or anything.

Try not to panic. Think as calmly as you can about how you will be able to escape. Creating the moment when you can escape is probably the only good reason for physically resisting a rapist. You probably have with you things which you can use to throw your attacker off guard: a lighted cigarette; a hatpin; tips of your keys, held between your fingers; a rolled newspaper or magazine that can be jabbed into his groin; a nail file.

Remember, if you are attacked your greatest defense is attracting attention. Scream — loud and long. Holler for help. Yell "Fire!" Make noise enough to bring assistance.

If Raped, What to Do

For many rape victims, reporting the ordeal is almost as much of a nightmare as the experience itself. But it is absolutely vital that you report a rape, both to protect yourself and to aid the police in catching the rapist. Many big city police departments have special rape units, with female officers with whom you can talk. Do not be timid; report this violent assault immediately.

Go to the police without cleaning yourself. Report all details of the attack, no matter how intimate. Try to recall anything unusual about the attacker — physical description, how he talked, what he said. Show the police external bruises and injuries. It's a good idea to show a friend or relative, too, and to have pictures taken, for possible evidence at a trial. Have someone bring you a change of clothing in case you have to leave any garments as evidence.

Then go to the nearest doctor or emergency room for an internal and external examination. Do not wash or douche until you have been examined. Tell the doctor precisely what happened so medical evidence of the attack can be noted. The doctor will try to take semen smears and, of course, will treat any bruises or injuries.

Later you should be checked for venereal disease or pregnancy. It may be a good idea to be accompanied by a police officer when you have a gynecological examination.

Going to court may be very trying, but it is necessary to stand up against this unspeakable assault. You'll have to be prepared to establish firmly that your experience was actually a rape and not a case of seduction or enticement. A rape trial is not a pleasant experience, but there is no other way to be sure of putting a rapist behind bars. But even if you're not willing to face a trial, you should report a rape to the police. You may provide evidence that will help other victims come forward with information that can mean an arrest and conviction.

Chapter 14

Protecting Your Children

For most people, their children are the most precious treasures in their lives. In many ways they are the most difficult to protect. However, we have more experience in this direction than in any other area of our personal security.

For your children's protection, know what they are doing and where, whom they are seeing. Give them strict rules as to the hours when they must be home. The nighttime is no time for a young person to be roaming the streets. This is particularly true for girls.

If your child leaves a meeting or a party after dark, he should call home before leaving. Better still, pick up your child personally or arrange to have someone you know drive him home.

Teaching Your Children to Avoid Trouble

If you want to keep children out of trouble, the place to start is in the high chair, both in terms of what they should not do and in terms of whom they should avoid.

Fundamental rules should be impressed on a child, along with a sense of the dangers involved. For example, any approach by a stranger should be reported to you or a school authority immediately.

A child should know his home address and phone number. He should know details of where his father and mother work, and where nearby relatives live.

Very young children should carry an address or identification card with them, with home address and telephone number clearly indicated.

Basic Rules for a Child

A child must be taught the following specific rules and guidelines:

1. Do not accept favors from strangers.
2. Never stand close to the car of a stranger who asks directions. Stand back several feet from it.
3. Do not ever hitchhike or accept a ride from a stranger.
4. Write down the license number of the car of any stranger who takes a friend for a ride or who asks you to come along. Use chalk or a stone, or scratch it in the dirt with a stick.
5. Do not play alone in alleys or near empty or deserted buildings or in out-of-the-way places.
6. Don't go into any buildings or rooms with strangers, for any reason.
7. A teen-ager must be told to avoid parking in deserted "lovers' lanes" or other secluded areas.

Teach your children to avoid hard liquor and smoking, even though you yourself may drink and smoke. You can explain that you do so in moderation and that the habits are ones you control and may even try to break. Discourage your children from experimenting with drugs. Some insight into the drug scene and some commentary on the effects of drug abuse are covered later on in this chapter.

Baby-Sitting

If your child is baby-sitting, make sure that you know the baby's family. Take your daughter or son over for the first baby-sitting session and take a good look at the family. Determine if any other adult will be in the home with your young child.

If you have someone baby-sitting for you, take the time to issue some basic, specific instructions on his or her expected behavior. For example, the baby-sitter should not use your phone except in an emergency. Here is an example of basic information and instructions:

Information for the Baby-Sitter
(complete and place near phone)

Important Telephone Numbers:

Police _____ or call Operator
Fire Dept. _____
Doctor (   ) _____
   or
Doctor (   ) _____
Ambulance _____
Neighbor, Mrs. _____
You Can Reach Us At:

_____ until _____
_____ until _____
_____ until _____

Here are some further instructions for your baby-sitter:

Do not allow anyone in the house except _____

Do not unlock the doors or windows.

Do not have visitors.

Do not tell anyone you are alone. Never respond on the phone, "I'm the baby-sitter." Say, "I'm a friend of the family." And volunteer no information except to say that the parents are expected back "very shortly."

Do not leave the house unattended. If an emergency arises, call for help.

Do not give any medication to the children except with specific instructions from us or a doctor.

Do not tie up the phone after you've made
the emergency call. Stay off the line.

Look in on the children after they fall
asleep.

Report anything unusual, like a prowler, to
the police.

Call us if you have any questions as to what
to do.

Check Out Your Baby-Sitter

Because most people think that they know those
they choose for baby-sitters, there is a special
hazard. They are usually a neighbor's kids or
friends of neighbors, nice old ladies, or people you
have known for years. What you may not know is
the special pressures they may be experiencing
financially, personally, and psychologically. In a
practical sense, there is not much you can do except
select your baby-sitter with great care and after a
proper interview.

Since you are letting a stranger into your house,
do not leave tempting articles around. You should
generally exercise the kind of care discussed in
earlier chapters on how to protect your valuables. Be
sure that your baby-sitter does not have any visitors
in the form of boyfriends or girlfriends, as they can
turn out to be light-fingered. Seek an older baby-
sitter or a young person with some maturity because
your baby-sitter is as vulnerable as your children or
yourself when in your home on his or her own.

Teach Respect for Police

Teach your children to respect the police and law-
enforcement agencies. Some parents use the police
as boogeymen, saying, "If you don't behave, I'll
have you arrested and taken to jail." This inhibits
children from turning to the police if they need help.
It creates a bad attitude toward men and women
who fundamentally exist to help in crisis situations.

Keeping Crime Out of the Family

Teen-agers tend to be antiestablishment and propeer. It is certainly not unusual for them to get involved in pranks, even shoplifting, the use of marijuana, alcohol, or taking chances while driving.

A child's teen years cover the time when a parent has to be particularly observant and has to work hardest to maintain an openness and rapport with his children to insure that they do not go astray. It is important to know who their friends are and to channel them into positive leisure activities.

Looking for Bad Signs

Some danger signals may indicate that a young person is straying from the straight and narrow path: (1) if his friends get into trouble; (2) if he has more possessions than his known income warrants; and (3) if he talks about visiting stores and places where he would not logically make purchases or which attract bad types of individuals.

Drugs as a Problem

Even a happy, well-organized home can fall prey to a drug problem, but the chances are less than in disrupted families. Drug addiction and alcoholism are often found among young people who have poor communication with their parents. The cause may be a lack of caring and concern by parents who do not fulfill their responsibilities.

How can you tell if your child is on drugs? Some of the indications include:

1. Watering eyes and nose.
2. Loss of appetite.
3. Dilated eyes.
4. A "high" that is more than just good spirits.

5. Brown stains on fingers.
6. Sores on arms or legs.
7. Lethargy, unresponsiveness, nervousness.
8. Short temper, bursts of anger.
9. Exaggerated responses, laughing, crying.
10. Loss of interest in grades, schools, personal appearance.
11. Twitching, diarrhea, vomiting, sleeplessness.
12. Hallucinations, convulsions, withdrawal.
13. And, if you look, finding drugs in your youngster's room is a solid piece of evidence. (They may be left around openly in the hope you will find them and show some interest!)

What Are Illegal Drugs?

Among the drugs that are most commonly available and are used illegally or which are themselves illegal are: heroin, marijuana, hallucinogens, cocaine, amphetamines, barbiturates, LSD, and methadone.

Early Signs

Glue sniffing is a common early sign of future trouble. It is nonaddictive, but dangerous to users. It can produce liver damage and anemia. Sniffing of Carbona, turpentine, and gasoline is also dangerous. These activities are signals of personality problems that cannot be ignored.

Is Drug Addiction Hopeless?

No!
Addiction can be ended, but early discovery and diagnosis is vital. Parents and friends must look for signs of the drug's effect, and steps must be taken to convince the youngster to give up the abuse of drugs.

Pill-Popping — The Abuse of Regular Drugs

Your prescription medication, either barbiturates or amphetamines, may be taken by children from your medicine cabinet. It is absolutely vital always to keep all medicines out of reach of children. Pill-popping is no laughing matter. It can lead to serious consequences and even death.

What to Do If Your Child Is on Drugs

First, prepare yourself psychologically for a pretty rough time. You are going to need patience and understanding. Then arm yourself with knowledge about the problem. Read current literature about drugs, so that you can speak knowledgeably and confidently with your child. You will need to know his language and recognize what he is describing and talking about when he uses common street expressions for various drugs.

Get professional help from a doctor, a psychiatrist, a clergyman, or even the police. In many areas, school counsellors or the police have proven to be extremely effective because they deal with the drug problem so frequently. If your police department's drug-abuse squad is a sympathetic and informed one, you may find it to be your great initial help.

There are clinics, both private and public, in many areas, which help parents and their children deal with the problem, which, of course, is both physical and psychological. Do not try to cope all by yourself. Get some help and try to work things out with your child. Above all, remain calm and keep open the lines of communication between your child and yourself.

Kidnapping

Fortunately, kidnapping is a rather rare occurrence. But it happens frequently enough — and to

ordinary people — to justify a word or two here
about how to prevent or avoid it. The following simple precautions will help:

1. Avoid publicizing your personal activities and
   schedules, and those of your family. Do not
   encourage the release of this kind of information, at home or in the office.
2. Keep your home secure.
3. If you think you may be a kidnapping target,
   arrange for your children to be escorted to
   and from school by a trusted adult.
4. Instruct school officials and other activity
   leaders (Boy Scouts, HiY, etc.) not to release
   your child to anyone other than a parent or
   an authorized person known to the child.

If You Are Kidnapped

A few basic thoughts may save your life. Teach
them to your children, and it could save theirs, too.

1. Try to stay calm. Don't panic.
2. Cooperate. Don't threaten.
3. Note as much about what is going on as you
   can: who is involved, where you are, what is
   happening, how to describe the kidnappers.
4. Escape by any means possible, should the opportunity arise.

Final Thoughts

As always, maintaining a calm approach to a
serious life-threatening problem can work miracles.
You can always collapse *after* the problem is resolv-
ed, but by keeping your wits about you and teaching
your children how to deal with such a situation, you
can do much to protect and preserve their lives and
your own.

Chapter 15

The Thief You Have Invited In

It is one thing to anticipate the thief seeking to break in from outside — but quite another to be guarded with seemingly "friendly" people close at hand.

The Con Artist

Do not open the door to trouble. Be suspicious from the start of schemes that seem to promise you something for nothing, that will make you rich quick, that will put any of your money into the hands of a stranger, even if only for a few minutes, or which may put you in a position where a packet of money can be switched.

The chief advantage the confidence man has is that "there's a little larceny in everyone." Remember, the con artist doesn't look like a thief. The whole idea is to separate you from your money through trickery and deceit. These culprits can be either men or women, working alone or in pairs, or even in groups. They may be well dressed. (Luxury hotels are often robbed by thieves in tuxedos! That doesn't make them any less heartless and devious.)

Such people may stop you on the street, call on the phone, or ring your doorbell. They may pretend to be repairmen, building inspectors, or assume any other identity. There are many different kinds of confidence games and new ones being invented every day.

The variations in confidence games are as great as people's imagination. While many of these schemes seem obvious in outline, *they continue to succeed* because there are people naive enough to believe they can get something for nothing, and because they are uninformed and trusting enough to let a con artist deceive them. Here's how three common ruses work.

The "Pigeon Drop"

A stranger, often a woman, begins a friendly conversation with you on a downtown street. A newcomer arrives, telling of finding a large sum of money. A discussion follows about what to do with it. The newcomer, claiming to work for a lawyer, says she will ask him what should be done with the money. When she returns from the attorney's office, she reports that the cash probably belonged to someone who wanted to conceal its existence to avoid taxes. Since she found it, she should keep it. However, since all three of you now know about it, the money would best be divided among you.

You and your stranger "friend" are asked to demonstrate that you have good-faith money, to justify sharing in this windfall. The stranger says she will draw some money out of her bank and show it to the lawyer, to prove her worthiness. She goes off and comes back a while later, stating that the lawyer gave her one-third of the found money.

Now the new friends ask you for your proof of money-worthiness. You all go to the bank where you are asked to withdraw several thousand dollars in cash. The lawyer's employee says she will take your money to the lawyer and return it with your share of the loot.

She returns and reports that the lawyer is satisfied. He wants you to come to his office to pick up the good-faith money and your one-third of the found money. You follow the intricate instructions to the lawyer's office, only to find that no such person or address exists. You have been swindled out of your money . . . through one of the oldest and most frequent ruses in the business.

The Envelope Switch

A man, sometimes with a foreign accent, approaches you for assistance. He tells you a plausible story about settling an estate for a relative who has just died. He doesn't know the area very well and the hotel he was supposed to go to doesn't exist any more. He shows you a large sum of money, in an envelope he's carrying, and he offers to pay you for your assistance.

A stranger happens by and states that the man should put that kind of money in a bank. The man says he doesn't trust banks. When you agree with the stranger that banks are indeed safe, the first man says he'll be persuaded if you can prove the safety of banks by withdrawing your money "any time you want it."

The three of you go to your bank and you make a withdrawal in cash. The first man insists that you hold his money, asking you to be especially careful. The newcomer suggests that you put your money in the same envelope as the first man's. You do that, seal the envelope and put it in your jacket pocket. The first man then tells you he will show you how *he* would protect the money, by putting it in a special pocket in his coat. You hand him the envelope which he places in this special pocket.

When you ask for the money back, he cheerfully returns the envelope to you from that special pocket. The two men excuse themselves for a moment. When they do not return, you grow concerned about giving the first man his money back. You open the envelope and discover that it contains only dollar-bill size pieces of newspaper or play money. It is a different envelope, and you have given your money away.

The Bank Examiner

You get a telephone call from someone who describes himself as a bank examiner or a policeman on the trail of some irregularity at your bank. A teller is suspected of some dishonest dealings and you are asked to cooperate in setting a trap for the culprit.

The examiner asks you to go to your bank, make a withdrawal in cash from a certain window, put the money in a special envelope and give it to him. When you do this, he gives you a receipt and tells you that the money will be redeposited in your account the next day, after the teller's records have been checked.

When you return to the bank in a few days to have your bankbook adjusted or to check on the redeposit, you find that no money has been put back in your account. There are no irregularities at the bank and no one with any authority has asked you to help. Your receipt is a worthless scrap of paper. You have been conned out of your money.

> *Note:* There are no occasions or circumstances when you will be asked by any legitimate authority — banking or police — to withdraw money from a bank and hand it over to anyone. Do not be taken in by this ploy.

The Better Business Bureau offers these tips to avoid being taken:

If an advance fee is required, be cautious.

Do not fall for vanity and get-rich-quick schemes. If it's flattery you get, consider the source.

Do not believe a guarantee of performance claim unless the company puts it in writing, signed by an officer.

Do not believe everything you read and do not expect newspapers or magazines to stand behind their advertisers' claims. They don't have to and most will not.

Do develop a healthy, informed skepticism and do not let a con-man lead you to abandon your experience and common sense to make you part with your money.

When you are vulnerable, out of a job, short of cash, or having family problems, do not fall for a scheme you would normally avoid if all your defenses were up.

Check with the Better Business Bureau or a local consumer agency to determine past experience with any firms you do not know.

People in Your Hire

Remember, too, that a theft may be encouraged, even planned, by a person who enters your house for a seemingly legitimate reason. Information is easily passed on as to the location of valuables, alarm systems, unprotected entranceways, and the times you will be away.

Be Cautious about Repairs

If you are having work done around the house, there is a special hazard. Deal with companies you know to be reliable. Check your valuables before and after they have begun to work. Check your security system after they are gone. If there is a risk of major loss, consider having someone around all the time they are working.

Employees Who Leave Can Be a Problem

Parting can be sour sorrow if someone in your hire leaves angrily or dissatisfied, or just suddenly departs for reasons unknown.

There are several things you should do immediately. Consider changing the locks on your doors. Change the places where you hide your jewelry or other valuables. Check your most valued possessions in case you must make an insurance claim. See that all the checks in your checkbook are accounted for. Examine the points in your whole security system which may be vulnerable.

Especially vulnerable are cash, jewelry, coins, appliances, stereos, television sets, firearms, liquor, and securities. Make sure they are not temptingly available to someone who knows you, your habits, and your possessions.

Make Sure You Check People's References

How do you protect yourself against theft by a cleaning woman, a baby-sitter, a live-in housekeeper, or a caretaker who has access to the house while you are away from home?

The only practical method is by checking references. Find out where the person has worked before, if he or she was let go, and if so, why.

When you have a new cleaning woman, cook, maid, handyman or baby-sitter, speak personally to the person given as a reference. Find out how he or she knows your new employee, for how long, and in what connection.

Spotting Counterfeit Money

One of the monopolies reserved only for the United States government is the printing of money. Counterfeiters have tried over the years to go into competition with Uncle Sam in this department, but invariably they are caught. You can help protect the integrity of your paper money by making sure that the money you handle is genuine, and by knowing what to do should you find yourself with a counterfeit bill.

It is not all that difficult to tell a fake bill from a real one, but since some counterfeits are extremely well done, it helps to know what to look for and how to spot a bad bill.

Workmanship: There are four main places to check:

> *The portrait* of a genuine bill stands out sharply from the background. The eyes are lifelike and the background screen is regular with beautifully even lines. On a counterfeit bill,

PORTRAIT

(Genuine)  *(Counterfeit)*

> the eyes are likely to be dull or smudged. The background lines are irregular, with some broken. The face may be less finely detailed than on a genuine bill.
>
> *The seal* of a genuine bill will have even and very sharp sawtooth points around the rim.

SEAL

(Genuine)   *(Counterfeit)*

> On a counterfeit bill, the sawtooth points may be blunt, uneven or broken.
>
> *Serial numbers* of genuine bills are firmly and evenly printed, and very evenly spaced. On counterfeit bills, the numbers may be poorly spaced, printed darker or lighter than normal, and unaligned. On Federal Reserve notes, the prefix letter may not agree with the district letter in the seal.

SERIAL NUMBERS

(Genuine)   *(Counterfeit)*

F 93310058 A   B 86733513 A

Scrollwork: In a legitimate bill, the fine lines are sharp and clean. A counterfeit bill's lines may be blurred and broken.

SCROLL WORK

(Genuine)   *(Counterfeit)*

Paper: Genuine bills are printed on paper of extremely high quality. Small blue and red threads in the paper are clearly visible in newer bills, but you will have to look harder for them in older or worn money. Counterfeit paper does not contain such threads. Tiny imitating lines may be printed or inked on the bill. Counterfeit paper has a different feel from authentic bills, and may be whiter, and less "alive-looking" than genuine paper.

Ink: You cannot tell a fake bill from a real one by rubbing it. The ink of either can be rubbed off. Colors of genuine bills may also vary considerably.

What to Do If You Get a Counterfeit Bill

Write your name and the date on the bill, so you can identify it later.

Write down the details of how you received it. From whom? When? Where? Under what circumstances?

Get in touch immediately with one of the following and explain the situation: the U.S. Secret Service; a Federal Reserve Bank; any commercial bank; or your local police.

It Is Up to You to Protect Yourself

Plain, good common sense and the exercise of reasonable caution in your dealings with others can do more than anything else to keep you safe and sound. You can shield yourself with alarms, and you can padlock your possessions with chains. But if you neglect your instinctive feelings, you can be headed for trouble.

It is nice to be trusting, but there are some people who are out to cheat and harm you. You have got to be wary of them.

It is nice to think of earning easy money, but you know in your heart that you do not get something for nothing. You have to learn to be suspicious of anyone who offers to give you valuables for no apparent reason.

It is nice to live an open, unsuspecting, trusting life, but those who do leave themselves open to others who would take advantage of them.

You can be nice, but safe at the same time, by being alert and sensible and calm.

Chapter 16

Fire Security

Home is where *nine out of ten* people die in fires! The *night hours* are the deadliest, when your senses are asleep and fire has plenty of time to build undetected. Most people, a third of them children, suffocate from poisonous fumes and smoke, overwhelmed in sleep, or in a panic of confusion and darkness.

Few people truly know of the extent of the threat, or the steps to take to protect their lives and their loved ones.

> *"For George and Viola Deutsch it was the best bargain that $48 could buy. When their furnace acted up last spring, the Portland couple purchased a smoke detector and placed it in a hallway near their children's bedrooms. A month later, a shrill alarm from the device awakened the couple. George Deutsch ran upstairs to discover that a fallen lamp had ignited one child's bedroom. He grabbed the sleeping boy from his flaming bed and led his wife and two other sons to safety. 'My husband thanks God he had enough initiative to get the smoke detector,' says Mrs. Deutsch. 'Otherwise we believe we would no longer have three sons.' "*
>
> — Newsweek

The National Fire Protection Association tells us that 75 percent of dwelling fires start as slow, smoldering fires. The resulting fumes, carbon monoxide, smoke and lack of oxygen are the killers — not the flames, as many might think.

WHERE FATAL RESIDENTIAL FIRES START

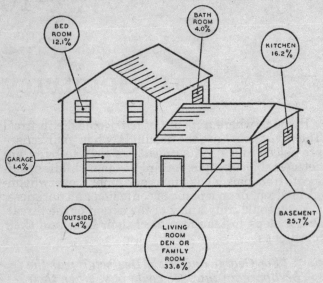

Courtesy of National Fire Protection Association

In a full-scale bedroom fire test sponsored by the National Science Foundation, *flashover* — complete involvement of a room and all its combustibles in flame — occurred just *seven minutes* after the start of the fire. And actually, after only *five minutes*, chances for survival would have been very small *because of the toxic fumes.*

Irritants released by burning common materials:

Wood:	Wool:	Rubber:	Plastics:
Carbon monoxide	Carbon monoxide	Carbon monoxide	Carbon monoxide
Carbon dioxide	Hydrogen sulfide	Hydrogen sulfide	Carbon dioxide
Formaldehyde	Sulfur dioxide	Sulfur dioxide	Hydrogen chloride
Formic acid	Hydrogen cyanide		Aldehydes
Carbolic acid	Ammonia		Ammonia
Methyl alcohol			Cyanide
Acetic acid			Nitrogen oxides

Smoke Alarms
Revolutionize Personal Security

Practical, low-cost smoke detection in the home is a recent development of science and technology. No satisfactory protection was available before this breakthrough. As a result, few people are sufficiently aware that *smoke,* not flame, is the menace that kills most fire victims. Smoke alarms dramatically change the odds in favor of your safe escape.

Now, with such an effective, inexpensive answer, the thing we need most is an *informed public* that will quickly take the three simple steps necessary to safeguard their lives. (1) Install early warning smoke alarms outside family bedrooms where the detectors will intercept the airborne products of combustion and sound a loud alarm before fumes can reach you. (2) Follow the escape planning advice included with all approved smoke alarms. (3) Always sleep with bedroom doors tightly closed to prevent deadly fumes from creeping up on you while your senses are asleep.

The U.S. Department of Housing and Urban Development now requires that a smoke detector be installed in all new homes backed by Federal Housing Administration (FHA) loans. The *FHA Minimum Property Standards Section 405-14 Fire Alarm Systems* reads:

> "*Not less than one* automatic smoke detector, which may be a single-station alarm device, shall be installed in each living unit near the sleeping areas. For two story dwellings one smoke detector in the upper hall at head of stairway is sufficient when the stairway is open and the lower sleeping area, if any, is adjacent to the open stairway."

Smoke detectors, important in all homes, are even more vital in mobile homes, small apartments, and small houses, which quickly fill with lethal smoke and fumes even from a small fire.

The basic choice is between ionization and photoelectric detectors. Each has slightly different advantages:

The ionization type uses a very small amount of radioactive material, usually Americium 241, which changes the air inside the detector into a conductor of electric current. If smoke enters the chamber, the particles mix with the ionized air, reduce current flow, and set off the alarm.

Photoelectric detectors use a light-sensitive cell as the sensor. A built-in light source directs its beam within the smoke chamber, but not onto the cell. If smoke enters, the particles reflect light onto the cell. And this triggers the alarm.

Which Alarm Is Best?

Neither ionization nor photoelectric has a clear-cut superiority over the other. Both types are approved by authorities. But there is a difference in speed of detection, depending on the type of fire.

It is the consensus that ionization is somewhat faster with flaming fires which may produce little or no visible smoke. Photoelectric responds to smoldering fires more quickly.

Ionization alarms usually are battery powered, since they require little current. This allows a great deal of freedom in mounting the alarm — an electrical outlet is not needed. However, periodic battery replacement is required (usually once a year).

Photoelectric alarms generally must be connected to electrical outlets. However, newer low-power-drain, solid-state designs allow photoelectric detectors to be battery operated. So the power-supply difference is fast passing into history, and your choice can be made on other factors.

A more desirable feature now becoming available (although it requires some handyman skills) is interconnection of units so that when any detector senses smoke, the others in the home also sound an alarm.

Do Ionization Alarms Pose a Radiation Hazard?

The radiation level of an approved ionization detector is typically too low to measure at the exterior surfaces of an ionization detector enclosure, according to Factory Mutual's Approval Department, an independent, widely recognized testing laboratory. The U.S. Nuclear Regulatory Commission reports that the radiation level derived from an approved ionization smoke detector is much less than from the normal environment which includes exposure to the sun and watching television. In fact, *normal surroundings* expose you to 200 times the radiation you would get from living with a smoke detector.

Semiconductor gas sensors have been omitted from consideration here as a practical smoke alarm. Although they operate from gasses driven off by fires and are low in cost, they are not fully tested long-term, and already have shown an annoying tendency to respond to gases having no connection with combustion, causing annoying false alarms.

What about "Heat Detectors"?

Most heat detectors are set to go off at 135° F. Some activate the alarm in response to a very rapid rise in temperature. As a result, heat sensors are effective *only in the presence of high temperatures*. Unlike smoke sensors, *they are not enough to protect life in bedroom areas* simply because they would not be an early warning device there. Heat sensors can provide a good secondary system for raising the overall level of protection, and should be located in rooms with a fireplace, in kitchens, or furnace-room areas.

Check the Label

Whatever fire detection device you use should carry the approval of an NFPA-recognized national testing service, such as Underwriters Laboratories, or Factory Mutual.

A Few More Tips on Smoke Alarms

To avoid nuisance alarms do not install a smoke detector in the kitchen or a room with a fireplace, in the garage, or so close to a furnace that it will be triggered by normal backdrafts.

Beware of the dangerous "human element". All battery-operated alarms will sound an intermittent warning signal when their batteries run low. **Do not silence the signal by disconnecting the power,** intending to replace the battery later, and then forgetting it! This neglect could be fatal, since you are without alarm protection under such conditions.

Smoke Detectors Are Only One Aspect of Fire Protection

The ideal protection is eliminating as many hazards as possible: flammable liquids carelessly stored in the basement, smoking in bed, careless use of space heaters.

A study by the NFPA shows the following causes of fatal residential fires: smoking — 56 percent; faulty heating equipment — 13.8 percent; faulty wiring — 7.5 percent; cooking stove — 7 percent; arson — 4.3 percent; all other sources — 11.4 percent.

How to Make Your Home Safer
*Tips from the
National Fire Protection Association*

Before a Fire Starts
• Close the doors to bedroom when you go to bed

- Have an escape plan, with a normal exit, and an alternate one
- Set up a place to meet after your family escapes
- Try your escape plan, and keep practicing it frequently
- Inspect appliances, stoves, and heaters for wear and unsafe or erratic operation
- Get an approved home fire detection and alarm system
- Don't leave young children alone
- Don't smoke when you are lying down, or when your judgment is impaired by fatigue, medicine, or alcohol

After a Fire Starts
- Rouse all occupants immediately
- Get out of the building immediately
- Get the whole family together and keep them together — don't go back in the building
- Call the fire department

Plan Your Safe Escape

Escape routes should be carefully planned in advance. Everyone needs to be drilled on how to act if fire strikes. Ask yourself these questions right now:

What if everyone is asleep?

What if the primary escape route is blocked by fire or dense smoke?

What if a baby-sitter is in charge of the house?

Intelligent planning is absolutely essential for a safe household. The obvious answer to question number one is that you need a smoke alarm to waken you. Question number two indicates the importance of having at least two ways out of every bedroom, usually a door and a window. Make sure that this escape window is not barred or obstructed, and is easy to open. If it is more than ten feet above the ground, you should have some means of getting to the ground such as a chain ladder or rope ladder (which can be inconspicuously stored under your bed), or an outside fire escape.

Special plans should be made for evacuating those who cannot escape by themselves.

As for question number three, you should make certain that baby-sitters know what to do: first gather up children (and do not waste time dressing them); then get them *outside the home* quickly. Once outside, close doors behind you. Keep the children *together* to make certain no one tries to reenter to save things. Then — and only then — summon the fire department from the nearest neighbor's phone, or an alarm box.

Detailed instructions are available from the National Fire Protection Assoc:, 60 Batterymarch Street, Boston, Mass. 02110. Request the "Babysitters Handbooklet for Emergency Action."

Practice Can Prevent Panic

Be sure to practice your emergency escape plan. See that children can actually open and escape from the window you expect them to use if the normal way out is blocked. Do not expect too much of children, but at least teach them to keep their bedroom doors closed and wait by an open window until someone can reach them.

Select a meeting place outside as part of your advance planning, so there won't be confusion and you will be certain that everyone is safely out of the home or building.

What if You Awaken to an Actual Alarm?

Stay calm.

Don't waste time getting dressed - move to safety *at once*.

Before you open your bedroom door, feel it to see

how warm it is. If it is hot, *do not open it.* If it is not, brace one foot and shoulder against the door, then open cautiously. Be prepared to slam it shut at the first hint of dense smoke or flame.

Follow your rehearsed escape plan, or use the alternate route if you must.

Call the fire department only from the safety of a neighbor's home.

Staying Alive in an Apartment-Building Fire

Even if you live in a modern apartment building of the finest fire-resistant construction, remember that you cannot know for sure just how fire resistant your building truly is and should not stay around inside to find out!

The time you must think about getting out is the moment you become aware of fire or smoke.

The fastest, safest way to get out is to use the normal exits. However, if heavy smoke and flames are blocking hallways and stairs, you may have to use a window or emergency exit.

DO NOT USE THE ELEVATORS. Elevator shafts are natural chimneys and may fill with poisonous smoke, fumes, and deadly heat. Power failure could imprison you roasting between floors. And some modern elevators were installed with heat sensitive controls to bring them to the floor with the fire. The idea here seemed good at the time: rush transportation to the floor most in need of it. But in practice the elevator may well take fleeing people from their own floor directly to a raging inferno, thanks to this automatic feature.

If the Door to the Corridor Is Hot

Feel the door to your apartment hallway before you open it. If it is hot, DO NOT OPEN IT. You may be engulfed in explosive flame the instant oxygen from your apartment meets the superheated gasses from the corridor. Do not plunge headlong down smoke-filled corridors either. One breath of highly toxic fumes may be enough to bring you down.

If your corridor is impassible, and conditions prevent you from reaching a stairway, close all the doors between you and the fire. Vents through which the smoke could reach you should be closed or blocked. Stuff jackets, clothing, towels, anything, under the door. Open a window — break one if you must — and get fresh air. Call the fire department from your apartment if the phone is working. Otherwise, shout like crazy to get someone in the street outside to pull an alarm.

If Someone Is Trapped

If people become trapped in a burning building before help arrives, you may be in a position to assist by summoning aid. But take great care in any direct personal action; measure with caution the danger to your life. A rescue attempt by an untrained person through heavy smoke or flames is virtual suicide. Do not try it.

Firemen are experts, specially trained and equipped to reach those trapped in burning buildings and to bring the victims and themselves out alive.

Another important point: watch your children if you have gotten out to be sure they do not go back in after a pet or favorite toy. This dangerous impulse has cost far too many young lives.

Selecting Fire Extinguishers for the Home

There are many fine fire extinguishers designed to fight small or beginning home fires. The immediate availability of a fire extinguisher can mean the difference between minor damage and total conflagration. This is especially true in the kitchen. However, don't waste time trying to use an extinguisher on a large fire. Get out, and call the fire department immediately.

When buying or using an extinguisher, you need to know that fires fall into three distinct categories. Class A fires occur in ordinary combustible materials such as wood, paper, cloth, and many plastics. They require an extinguisher with a Class A designation. Class B fires are those involving flammable liquids, gasses or grease. Class C fires involve live electrical equipment. Use the appropriate extinguishers for each type of fire. There is only one kind of home fire extinguisher (monammonium phosphate) rated to fight all three classes of fire. Carefully check the symbols on the extinguisher before buying or using one.

Class A and B type extinguishers also are categorized by their capacity for putting out fires. Each is marked with a number, and the higher the number, the greater the capacity. If the intention is protection against fire that might start in flammable liquids *and* electrical equipment, as in a kitchen, a B:C extinguisher designated at least 5-B:C is recommended. Where fire is apt to break out in ordinary combustible materials *and* in live electrical equipment (living room, bedroom), a multipurpose extinguisher with at least a 2-A:10-B:C minimum rating should be available.

Household Fire Safety Checklist

To see how well you're doing in achieving a "Fire Safe" home, answer the questions in this check list. Do it once a year to measure improvement (or worse, to determine if you and your family have become lax)! Skip questions which do not apply to you. The following is your Fire Safety index:

5 or more "NO" answers: You're in trouble!

3 to 4 "NO" answers: Improvement needed.

1 to 2 "NO" answers: Good, but you can still do better.

0 "NO" answers: Congratulations for maintaining a FIRE SAFE home!

ESCAPE

	Yes	No
1. Does everyone in your household recognize the importance of getting out immediately if they even suspect the existence of a fire?	☐	☐
2. Does everyone in your household know that life safety is the first consideration and that no actions (even calling the fire department) should be taken until after everyone has been alerted?	☐	☐
3. Have you shown everyone in your household the ways they can get out in case of fire? Do they know more than one way out?	☐	☐
4. Can all windows and doors needed for emergency escape be opened easily from the inside?	☐	☐
5. Does everyone in your household know which fire department to call if you live in a suburb or rural area?	☐	☐
6. Do you make it a regular practice to let your baby-sitters know what to do in case of fire?	☐	☐

HAZARDOUS MATERIALS

7. Is gasoline always opened, poured and used only outdoors?	☐	☐
8. Is all gasoline stored in either a UL labeled safety can or a capped metal can in a shed or garage?	☐	☐
9. If you have more than 1 gallon of gasoline stored, is it in a safety can?	☐	☐
10. Are other flammable liquids and combustible liquids either in their original containers or in tightly capped metal cans?	☐	☐

11. Do you take precautions never to use a ☐ ☐
combustible liquid to "freshen" any fire
nor to start a fire in a stove not designed
for liquid fuel?

FIRE EQUIPMENT

12. Are smoke detectors tested regularly as ☐ ☐
recommended by the manufacturer?

13. Have new batteries been installed in ☐ ☐
battery-operated smoke detectors within
the past year?

14. Have all fire extinguishers been check- ☐ ☐
ed and recharged according to instructions on the nameplate?

ELECTRICAL

15. Are all the fuses in your home the ☐ ☐
proper size? (15 or 20 amp on general circuits except special stove, dryer, or air-
conditioner circuits.)

16. Have you operated circuit breakers in ☐ ☑
your home several times each year to be
sure they don't stick?

17. Does the insulation on all electric cords ☐ ☐
appear to be in good condition?

18. Are the plugs and receptacles on all ☐ ☐
electric cords attached tightly and in good
condition?

19. Have all electric outlet and switch ☐ ☐
plates been checked within the past 6
months to determine whether they are hot
to the touch?

HEATING EQUIPMENT

20. Have you inspected the chimney this ☐ ☐
year to be sure there are no cracks or loose
bricks? Are metal chimneys well supported with tight connections?

21. Are the smoke pipes on all furnaces ☐ ☐
and heaters well supported, tightly connected and clear of combustibles?

22. Is combustible material kept at least ☐ ☐

three feet from your furnace, heaters, and stoves unless instructions permit lesser clearance?

23. Do you oil, clean, adjust, and perform other needed maintenance on heating equipment as required by the manufacturer's instructions?   ☐ ☐

HOUSEKEEPING

24. Are filled wastebaskets regularly emptied?   ☐ ☐

25. Do you keep matches and lighters away from small children?   ☐ ☐

26. Are ashes from smoking materials emptied into the toilet, the garbage disposer, or into a covered metal can?   ☐ ☐

27. Do you use ashtrays only on solid surfaces instead of on arms or seats of upholstered furniture?   ☐ ☐

28. Do you make a fire safety walk-through of your home before going to bed?   ☐ ☐

Chapter 17

Preparing for the Worst

Why didn't I?

After every robbery or fire that question pops up.

And the question that comes up most often is why did I not keep a record of all the things in the house.

Although this chapter is at the end of this book, it deals with things you should do first - before anything happens, almost as soon as you have moved into a home.

The Emergency List

The first of two clerical jobs you should do is establish a list of emergency numbers and facts. Do not depend on your memory. People have been known to forget their own name under pressure.

Type this suggested basic list on a card and tack it near your telephone. You will probably have additional names and numbers to add, once you start filling in these blanks.

Use the following guide to list the numbers you should have readily at hand in case of emergency.

EMERGENCY TELEPHONE NUMBERS

Your address _____

Police Department _____

Fire Department _____

Hospital _____

Doctor (office) _____

Doctor (home) _____

Local Rescue Squad _____

Pharmacy _____

Poison-Control Crisis Hotline _____
Emergency relative or best friend _____
Neighbors _____
Plumber _____
Gas Company _____
Electric Company _____
Taxi Company _____
Auto Insurer _____
Auto Insurance Policy Number _____
Husband's Office _____
Wife's Office _____
School _____

Tip: If you ever have a need to call the police or fire
department, you will want them to be able to identify your house quickly and easily. Make sure your
house number can be seen clearly from the street.

Your Personal Valuable Property Inventory

Next, you should make a complete and thoroughly
descriptive list of the things you have in your home.

If you have ever played the game "observation"
you know that no one can remember all the things
he has seen on a tray only a few minutes before. If
you ever have a loss, you will find it almost impossible to remember all the things you had. It will be
even harder to prove the loss to your insurance company or to the government for a tax deduction unless
you keep special records.

Your personal inventory is not just an ordinary
list. It should describe exactly what the item is, the
make or brand name, model number, color, any
serial number, the cost, when and where you
purchased it, and an estimated present value. An insurance company may also want to see purchase
bills, so save these, if you have them.

One of the best list accompaniments and insurance verifications is to take room-by-room
photographs. For easiest identification, take four
pictures in each room, standing with your back

against the center of each wall. These photos will serve as excellent memory joggers and will provide a positive record of your possessions. Caution: keep these prints or slides in your safety deposit box.

Identify Your Possessions

You can add to the value of the list by putting your own identification on each item. Your social security number or a number provided by your police department can be etched on most metal objects: television sets, radios, cameras. A silversmith will put an identifying hallmark on your valuable sterling. Furs can be marked indelibly on the inside skin itself, covered by the lining. Jewelry, antiques, works of art and cars should be photographed preferably from two or more angles.

Note location and type of identifying marks on your inventory list. Be sure to keep one copy in your safe-deposit box, the other in a convenient place where you will be able to find it for updating.

If you have a vacation home, do not forget to include all the personal property located there, too.

Be sure to update your list at a regular time each year. You will be surprised at how fast it changes. If you plan to review it around your birthday every year, you will always remember when to do it.

Know Your Insurance

Now that you know the value of your possessions, make sure that you have sufficient insurance to cover any loss.

Insurance companies sell many different types of homeowner's policies, numbered in sequence from HO-1 to HO-6. The higher the numbers, the better the coverage with generally, fewer exclusions . . . and, of course, the greater the cost. Policy HO-5 covers most risks. It is called the all-risk policy, in fact, but it still excludes certain hazards such as war or riots. The coverage generally is as follows:

HO-1. Fire and extended coverage, including burglary and theft.

HO-2. All the above, plus extended water and smoke damage.

HO-3. All-risk coverage of building, with named peril clause for contents.

HO-4. Apartment coverage.

HO-5. All-risk on building and contents.

HO-6. Special policy for condominiums and cooperatives.

In general, there are eighteen risks that the companies will insure against:

1. Fire, lightning
2. Property removed because it is endangered
3. Windstorm and hail
4. Explosion
5. Riot damage
6. Aircraft damage
7. Damage by vehicles now owned or operated by the insured person
8. Damage by smoke
9. Damage by vandalism and malicious mischief
10. Glass breakage
11. Theft
12. Falling objects causing damage
13. Damage from weight of snow or ice
14. Collapse of all or part of building
15. Bursting of hot-water pipe, plumbing, heating, or air conditioning equipment
16. Overflow of water from leaks
17. Freezing of plumbing, heating, or air conditioning equipment
18. Accidentally generated currents to appliances, fixtures and wires, but not tubes, transistors, and other electronic components

The policy numbers may vary from company to company and the details may be slightly different, but basically the policies are standard.

Risks Not Covered

There are some risks that insurance policies do not cover routinely, notably floods and earthquakes.

In some communities, special flood control measures required by the federal government have been completed. In these communities, the government arranges for flood insurance up to $35,000 on a home, and up to $10,000 on personal property, with the premium subsidized by the federal agency in charge.

How Much Insurance?

A basic element of your policy is how much insurance you should get in the homeowner's policy. The amount of insurance on your house and personal property depends largely on your own choice. Of course, the premium increases as your values increase. However, there is a maximum value on certain items unless you take out special coverage on these. These include:

1. Money, bullion
2. Stamp or coin collection
3. Bank notes
4. Securities
5. Manuscripts
6. Jewelry and furs
7. Boats, boat trailers, boating equipment
8. Trailers
9. Antiques
10. Artwork

A special policy can be obtained insuring these for greater amounts.

You may also get a floater insurance policy to protect any items such as cameras, tape recorders, and calculators which you carry with you on trips. No matter where such items may be stolen or lost, they are protected by the floater policy.

A policy may also provide for reimbursement for

the cost of living expenses if you cannot occupy your home.

Your insurance premium will depend on where you live, how your home is constructed, and of course, how much insurance you can afford or want to carry. In some areas, insurance companies will not insure you at all. If you have had several losses, some companies will refuse to insure you as a bad risk.

Most homeowners think in terms of what they paid for a home when they take out an insurance policy, but if the home burns down, it will be replaced at tomorrow's prices, considerably more than what you may have paid ten years ago or even last year.

If your community assesses property at full value, you can get an idea of the value of your house and land at a recent market price. You need insure only for the value of the home, of course, not for the land it is on.

Some insurance companies resolve the inflation factor by offering a policy that increases the value each year. The increase may be figured at a fixed percentage based on recent experience or tied to a construction cost as published by the U.S. Department of Commerce. Increases based on a fixed percentage are rarely adequate today as inflation has been growing and varies from year to year.

Coinsurance

Coinsurance is a mysterious factor to many insurers although it is a usual part of every homeowner's policy. The clause is designed to protect a company insuring a $50,000 house for $25,000 and paying out the full amount if there is $25,000 in damage. The clause requires that you insure for at least 80 percent of the true value of the property, otherwise the policy will pay only a proportionate share of the damages resulting from one of the covered risks.

In a situation where a homeowner insures for half the value and suffers damages of $20,000, he would receive 50/80th of the $20,000 or $12,500.

Inasmuch as inflation may have increased the value of your house so that you are covered for less than 80 percent of the true value, you should reevaluate your policy each time you renew it or more frequently if values in your area change drastically.

Personal Property

In addition to covering the replacement value of the house, the homeowner's policy covers personal property such as furniture, draperies, clothing, television, and stereo sets. The policy covers all property in the house, your own, borrowed, or anything stored there. There are some exceptions, such as an automobile in your garage, for example.

The insurance company and the insurer think of coverage on replacement costs. In most cases, personal property is valued at "actual cost value" . . . the value of the property immediately before a loss. Another way to figure is based on the purchase price less depreciation. The rate of depreciation varies from as little as 7 percent a year on furs, to 100 percent on such things as underwear, shirts, and shoes.

Problems will arise in valuing antiques and works of art. These should be carried separately on a fine arts policy with values specifically indicated and certified by an appraiser.

Alarm System Discounts

An alarm system will, of course, lessen the risk of theft and damage by fire for the insurance company as well as for yourself. Most companies will offer a discount on the premium if you have an intruder alarm system and an even larger one if you have a system that connects with the police station or a private protective agency. In some cases, the alarm system will induce an insurance company to accept a policy that would otherwise be rejected. A few companies also honor a fire-alarm system as a risk and premium reducing factor.

Government Insurance

If a private company won't give you an insurance policy, you may apply for a United States government policy of up to $10,000 against loss from burglary and robbery, if you live in Connecticut, Delaware, Florida, Illinois, Kansas, Maryland, Massachusetts, Missouri, New York, New Jersey, Ohio, Pennsylvania, Rhode Island, Tennessee, or the District of Columbia. Premiums run from $60 to $80 a year. For information, write Federal Crime Insurance, P.O. Box 41033, Washington, D.C. 20014. The government will insist that you have certain types of locks on your doors in order to be eligible.

Some companies have a reputation for quick settlement, others for delay. Try to find out before you subscribe for your policy. In any event, file your claim quickly. The sooner the process starts rolling, the sooner you will get paid.

If You Have a Loss

First, report the event to the police or fire department. Do not disturb anything after a robbery or a fire. Officials will want to see what happened, to try to find clues of the criminal event. If a fire is involved, insurance companies will want to see the damage and document it.

Report all stolen credit cards and note any blank checks that have been stolen. You must provide the insurance carrier with a list of damages and personal property stolen, with a schedule of costs. Most carriers will ask you to prove the costs with original bills or duplicate bills. The insurance company will deduct the depreciation from the costs, but will not add any appreciation to the values.

Here's where the value of your photos and personal property list shows up. The insurance company will require an inventory of what has been taken or damaged, and proof of purchase and cost. If you have to make a claim, the insurance form will ask for a full description of the property comprising the claim. You will need to know to whom it belonged; the replacement cost (including tax); the place where it was purchased (if it was a gift, the name and address of the giver); the allowance for depreciation in style, value, or wear and tear; the net value; and the amount of your claim for each item.

The time to get your records in order is NOW, before anything happens.

The Forcible Entry Clause

Most insurance policies require as part of the proof of loss, that proof of "forcible entry" be shown. This may be a broken window, a jimmied door, or even a scratch to show how an entry was made. Make sure you locate this point of entry and show it to the police.

Proving a Claim

Obviously, if you are burglarized or burned out, you must provide a good deal of proof before you can collect on your insurance.

Everything is going to require proof and the best proof in many cases, along with the lists and the bills you are preparing and saving, are photos, before and after the act of burglarizing or of theft. Photograph everything in addition to listing it.

Insurance claims may take anywhere from three months to three years to settle. There is much investigation, reporting, evaluation, and discussion before the amount is determined.

Do not be too quick to settle with a claims agent from your insurance company. It is possible that for months you will remember things you forgot to list among your losses. Make sure you know the full extent of your loss.

Be firm. You paid for good coverage. Make sure you get an adequate settlement. You may need the services of an attorney to support your claim and effort.

A Loss Is Deductible

As a last resort, your losses in excess of $100 for any individual robbery are a deductible item from your income when you file your income tax. This will take some of the edge off your loss.

If They Find Your Property

The police will circulate the descriptions of the property you report stolen. Whenever they find stolen property, they will try to match it with your descriptions. Sometimes they circulate the descriptions you give them to pawnbrokers and others.

If and when something turns up, your personal inventory and your list of identifying marks become very important. Without it, it will be difficult to pick your Polaroid from a half-dozen similar models picked up by the police in a raid . . or to prove it is yours even if you can identify it.

Be Prepared

Time spent now preparing an inventory of possessions and checking insurance coverage is an investment in the future that we hope you will never need to use. But, if the tragedy of fire or break-in does strike your home, your preparation will allow you to pull it through faster and easier. And, you won't be torn by the question "Why didn't I . . . ?"

A Final Word

So now you know! It really *can* happen to you. But it doesn't *have* to. Using the knowledge you have gained from these pages, you can significantly reduce the chance that you will become a crime statistic or victim.

It is all a question of preparing to meet the kinds of situations which can be dangerous and difficult. If you anticipate unexpected, but very possible, circumstances, and you take the precautions suggested here, you can go a long way toward preventing misfortune or even tragedy. With your increased sense of confidence and a secure certainty that you are doing everything possible to make your life safe, you will be much more likely to avoid difficulties and to overcome those which can not be averted.

And that is really the whole message of this book. The practical advice provides you with a kind of road map to follow. We have tried to point out some of the pitfalls and some of the opportunities that you should be aware of. Now it is up to you.

All the suggestions and advice and hints and recommendations in this book — or in any book — won't do any good unless you make the effort to *Protect Yourself*.

Index

Dell Bestsellers

REMEMBER IT DOESN'T GROW ON TREES

ENERGY CONSERVATION -
IT'S YOUR CHANCE TO SAVE, AMERICA
Department of Energy, Washington, D.C.